CHILDREN, TEENS, FAMILIES, AND MASS MEDIA

The Millennial Generation

LEA's Communication Series
Jennings Bryant / Dolf Zillmann, General Editors

Selected titles in Mass Communication (Alan Rubin, Advisory Editor) include:

Alexander/Owens/Carveth • *Media Economics: Theory and Practice, Second Edition*

Bryant/Bryant • *Television and the American Family, Second Edition*

Harris • *A Cognitive Psychology of Mass Communication, Third Edition*

Moore • *Mass Communication Law and Ethics, Second Edition*

Palmer/Young • *The Faces of Televisual Media: Teaching, Violence, Selling to Children, Second Edition*

Perse • *Media Effects and Society*

Price • *The V-Chip Debate: Content Filtering From Television to the Internet*

Van Evra • *Television and Child Development, Second Edition*

For a complete list of titles in LEA's Communication Series, please contact Lawrence Erlbaum Associates, Publishers at www.erlbaum.com

CHILDREN, TEENS, FAMILIES, AND MASS MEDIA

The Millennial Generation

Rose M. Kundanis
Keene State College

LAWRENCE ERLBAUM ASSOCIATES, PUBLISHERS
2003   Mahwah, New Jersey   London

Lawrence Erlbaum Associates, Inc., Publishers
10 Industrial Avenue
Mahwah, NJ 07430

Cover design by Sean Trane Sciarrone

Library of Congress Cataloging-in-Publication Data

Kundanis, Rose.
Children, teens, families, and mass media : the millennial generation / by Rose M. Kundanis.
    p. cm.
    Includes bibliographical references and index.
ISBN 0-8058-4563-1 (cloth : alk. paper)
ISBN 0-8058-4564-X (pbk. : alk. paper)
1. Mass media and children—United States. 2. Mass media and teen-agers—United States.   I. Title.
P94.5.C552U65   2003
305.23—dc21
                                                          2002044782
                                                                CIP

Books published by Lawrence Erlbaum Associates are printed on acid-free paper, and their bindings are chosen for strength and durability.

Printed in the United States of America
10 9 8 7 6 5 4 3 2 1

This book is dedicated to my students
at Keene State College whose interest in the topic
of children and media encouraged me to write this book,
and whose suggestions account for many of its strengths.

And to my daughter Zoe with whom I have shared
the delights of media from
Sesame Street to *Anne of Green Gables*.

Contents

PART III: EMPOWERING AUDIENCES

Preface

Children, Teens, Families, and Mass Media: The Millennial Generation provides a survey of the relationship of children and media using children's own experiences in addition to current theory and research concerning children from 2 to 18 years of age in the context of U.S. society and culture. The media of radio, television, and the Internet are the focus of this book, because these particular media are home utilities and therefore are those media most accessible to children regardless of age. The Millennial Generation—those children who graduated high school in the year 2000 and after—are the subject of the book as well as the intended audience. The text chapters have side bar interviews with teens who work in media and with people who develop policy or programming for children's media. The illustrations are taken from published comic strips and political cartoons as well as children's illustrations solicited specifically for this book.

Although many books are written as anthologies on the topic of children and media, this book is a monograph written for college undergraduates. Many books are written for a popular audience or for scholars and graduate students; this book however, is written in a variety of expository styles to provide clarity and models for undergraduate writing. The book is written in a research-paper style so as to model that type of academic writing. The writing style varies to include interview-based sections written in a more journalistic style. The writing is intended to provide models for academic and journalistic writing for the student audience. The book provides a glossary and questions and activities for further consideration to extend the exploration of topics in the classroom. Although many books provide adult art for illustrations, this book provides some illustrations by children in the age group this book is discussing. The book was written for a college-level course on children and the media. It also can be used as a supplemental text for courses such as Introduction to Mass Media, Mass Communication and Society, and Media Literacy. Other courses for which the text would be appropriate include areas in education, communication, psychology, and public health. The medical profession also sees children and the media as an important public health topic.

The approach is theory based with attention to developmental, gender, ethnic, and generational differences of children ages 2 to 18. Part I gives the theoretical context in chapters 1 to 3. Chapter 1 provides theories emphasizing various elements of the communication model. Chapter 2, the developmental theory chapter, is critical to the study of children and media because it discusses the issue of age differences, an issue that is often overlooked by the public. Many of the difficulties we have with the relationship of children and media occur because children's developmental differences are not taken into account. For example, it is crucial that children's inability to differentiate fantasy and reality before age 8 be established for our society. The inability to differentiate fantasy from reality can lead to behaviors such as children imitating violence without any concern for the reality or the consequences of the acts. Chapter 3 uses generational theory to provide a historic context based on people as well as events and changes in technology.

With a basis in theory, the focus shifts to the audience of children. Part II, Audience Reactions, examines children's perceptions of fantasy and reality (chap. 4), the effects they may experience (chap. 5), and the diverse identities (chap. 6) children may develop using media messages.

After this consideration of the child audience, Part III looks at what tools we have in the relationship of children and media. The last section, Empowering Audiences, reviews the various ways our society has of monitoring the relationship by examining the role of parents and families (chap. 7), the role of adults and schools in teaching media literacy (chap. 8), the role of society in developing policies and laws (chap. 9), and the role of programmers in listening to the audience (chap. 10). Chapter 9 presents the Children's Television Act of 1990, the Telecommunications Act of 1996, and various attempts at restricting indecency on the Internet. The related case law and Federal Communications Commission (FCC) regulations help to interpret and either support or eliminate laws passed by Congress. By including interviews with U. S. Representative Edward Markey and FCC Commissioner Susan Ness, the difficult legal concepts become easier for the reader to understand. Chapter 10 emphasizes the importance of listening to the audience in developing programming and includes several interviews with people working with *Sesame Street, Blue's Clues,* and *Nick News.* These provide a current view of children's programming as it is done today. Readers can understand the economic and programmatic variables that go into making long-lasting children's programming.

ACKNOWLEDGMENTS

Thanks to the many people at Keene State College (KSC) who have encouraged, supported, and helped me in completing this book: my colleagues Rita Miller, Sander Lee, Craig Brandon, David Payson, Mark Timney, Cheri Campbell, Shirley Smallman, and Diane Monahan; and KSC administrators and staff including

Robert Golden, Janet Gross, Michael Haines, Rita Miller, and Denvy Bowman. I had help from KSC Mason Library faculty and staff including Patrick O'Brien, Lois Merry, Marilee Rouillard, Judith Hildebrandt, and Anne Ames. Thanks to my student assistant Shaina Harlow for her organization skills, to Deb Edwards, Carol Fairbanks, and Jean Whitcomb who did funds administration, and to Joan Norcross who transcribed some of the interviews. Thanks to Vicki Moore for her music expertise.

Thanks for the collegial support off campus from Emily Edwards and Mary Ann Albertine. George Kundanis and Karen Lightfoot helped and supported me in many ways during my research trip to Washington, D.C. Thanks to the Keene Writers Group for their feedback and constructive criticism: Peter Allen, Lucie Germer, Jerry Germer, Travis Hiltz, Adrienne Spector, and Bruce Hesselbach.

Thanks to all those who generously gave of their time and expertise in interviews conducted in 1999–2000: Youth Communication Executive Director Bill Brooks; *New Expression* advisor Billy Montgomery and *New Expression* student staff Charles Scott and Dominique Washington; Reporter Leslie Baldacci, *Chicago Tribune* Family Editor Denise Joyce; Casey Journalism Center Director Beth Frerking and Casey Research Director Jenny Moore; *CentralXpress.com* producer Dan Oliver and student actors Hannah Slomianyj and Caitlin Wells; Kidsnet Executive Director Karen Jaffe; *20 Below* staff Melissa Kim Phillips and Jessica Tomlinson; U.S. Representative Edward Markey; FCC Commissioner Susan Ness; Sesame Workshop Chief Executive Office Gary Knell, *Sesame Street* Research Director Rosemarie Truglio, and *Sesame Street* Executive Producer Michael Loman; Nickelodeon Vice President of Worldwide Planning and Research Bruce Friend, *Blue's Clues* Creator Angela Santomero; *Blue's Clues* Research Director Alice Wilder; and *Nick News* producer Mark Lyons.

Thanks to all the hardworking schedulers who arranged for my interviews: Jill Lempke of Sesame Workshop, Mark Levine and Catherine Alcoran of Nickelodeon, David Moulton (Rep. Markey's office) and Lauren Northrop (Commissioner Ness's office).

Thanks to those who helped me to provide the art in this book. Anne Meddaugh worked hard with her art students at Wheelock School in Keene, New Hampshire: Devin Donohue, Christian Incandella, Cody MacLellan, Kelty McGonagle, Matthew Tacy and Jackie Todd. Graphic artist Catherine Hazelrigg did a beautiful job with the figures in chapter 1. *Blue's Clues* staff Catherine Alcoran and Geoff Todebush helped me with the *Blue's Clues* image. Sesame Workshop Studio Coordinator Gladys J. Easterling helped me to acquire the images of Cookie Monster and Elmo. Thanks to Universal Press Syndicate permissions coordinator Raegan Carmona, United Features Syndicate's Maura Peters, and Partnership for a Drug Free America's Josie Feliz.

Thanks to those at Lawrence Erlbaum Associates staff who were always accessible and patient: editors Linda Bathgate and Karin Wittig Bates, Promotion Coordinator Susan Barker, Senior Book Production Editor Sara T. Scudder, Production V.P. Art Lizza, and the meticulous work of copy editor Teresa Horton.

This book could not have been accepted without the thorough critique of reviewers, including Alison Alexander from the University of Georgia, whose work was a beacon of light guiding me to the end of this project.

Finally, all of the work would have been neither possible nor worthwhile without the loving support of my husband John and daughter Zoe during the long hours of research and writing.

—Rose M. Kundanis

PART I

Theoretical Context

CHAPTER ONE

Introduction

FIRST ENCOUNTERS

Think back to your childhood and your first encounter with a book, video, audio-cassette tape, film, television show, or Internet source. How did you perceive the experience? Wally Lamb (1992) begins his book *She's Come Undone* with Dolores's first encounter with television:

> In one of my earliest memories, my mother and I are on the front porch of our rented Carter Avenue house watching two delivery men carry our brand-new television set up the steps. I'm excited because I've heard about but never seen television. The men are wearing work clothes the same color as the box they're hefting between them. Like the crabs at Fisherman's Cove, they ascend the cement stairs sideways. Here's the undependable part: my visual memory stubbornly insists that these men are President Eisenhower and Vice President Nixon.
>
> Inside the house, the glass-fronted cube is uncrated and lifted high onto its pedestal. "Careful, now" my mother says, in spite of herself; she is not the type to tell other people their business, men particularly. We stand watching as the two delivery men do things to the set. Then President Eisenhower says to me, "Okay, girlie, twist this button here." My mother nods permission and I approach. "Like this," he says, and I feel, simultaneously, his calloused hand on my hand and, between my finger, the turning plastic knob, like one of the checkers in my father's checker set. (Sometimes when my father's voice gets too loud at my mother, I go out to the parlor and put a checker in my mouth—suck it, passing my tongue over the grooved edge.) Now, I hear and feel the machine snap on. There's a hissing sound, voices inside the box. "Dolores, look!" my mother says. A star appears at the center of the green glass face. It grows outward and becomes two women at a kitchen table, the owner of the voices. I begin to cry. Who shrank these women? Are they alive? Real? It's 1956; I'm four years old. This isn't what I've expected. The two men and my mother smile at my fright, delight in it. Or else, they're sympathetic and

consoling. My memory of that day is like television itself, sharp and clear but un-
reliable. (p. 4)

Lamb's description touches on several topics we will be exploring. How do
child and teen perceptions of television or any mass medium differ from the
perceptions of adults? Not only do youth perceptions differ from those of adults as
did those of Dolores from her mother, but they are different at various
developmental ages. The context for the relationship of children, teens, and the
media is presented in the first three chapters. The theoretical context is in this
chapter (chapter 1). The development of children's perceptions of mass media is
the topic of chapter 2, and the changes in media experiences by generations is the
topic of chapter 3.

What is real and what is fantasy? For 4-year-old Dolores, it was difficult to
differentiate the deliverymen from the images of President Eisenhower and Vice
President Nixon she later saw on the screen of the television. Stereotypical
perceptions are normal at age 4. In addition, children up to age 8 cannot differentiate fantasy from reality. For Dolores, stereotypes and difficulty distinguishing
fantasy from reality caused her to be fearful. Moving the television into the house
was Dolores's earliest memory. The physical placement of media utilities in the
home and their function in the home can have an effect just as a perception can
make the child afraid. The next three chapters examine how children, teens, and
families react to mass media with perceptions of fantasy and reality (chapter 4),
effects (chapter 5), and identity (chapter 6).

How can children better use the mass media as tools for their own empowerment? Dolores described the media's "sharp and clear" pictures in contrast to their
"reliability." Chapters 7, 8, and 9 examine the mediation of families (chapter 7),
schools through media literacy (chapter 8), and government and other policymakers (chapter 9). In the concluding chapter (chapter 10), we look at children's
programming and the industry that creates it.

DEFINITIONS AND CENTRAL IDEAS

Children and teen years are defined here as ages 2 to 18. Treating children as a
separate developmental group is a fairly recent concept.

> While children are mentioned in the Bible and in the writings of Plato, the idea that
> they ought to be protected, catered to and nurtured is a fairly recent notion in public
> discourse. That they are a constituency of the media in all of its functions—news
> and information, opinion, entertainment and marketing—is itself rather revolu-
> tionary. (Dennis & Pease, 1996, p. xix)

Although modern culture views children as a separate group to be nurtured,
children and teens are not passive in the process. Rather, they are active in using

mass media as part of their own socialization. When the dominant mass medium was print, children had to learn how to read before gaining access to information and entertainment. That barrier does not exist in the mass media of film, radio, television, video, and Internet. This accessibility of electronic media has brought the problems of the larger world into our homes and challenged the role of parents in raising children. Although we have viewed children as a separate group in personal nurturing, society also has made exceptions for children in law and regulations. However, for mass media, only guidelines and voluntary arrangements persisted until the Children's Television Act of 1990 (see chapter 9, "Policy and Law").

Mass media are those channels of communication that reach the wider audience simultaneously with their messages. Although print media are mass media, the focus here will be on the electronic home utilities of radio, television (and variations including broadcast, cable, satellite, video, and DVD), and the Internet. Film is an outside-the-home medium except as it is found on video. Being available only outside the home, film requires cost and sometimes transportation and adult supervision, which media inside the home do not. Mass media have become a home utility and with this home utility status, they seem to be challenging families as a primary socializing agent by bringing the larger world into our homes.

Children, teens, and families have a complicated relationship to mass media that varies with age, gender, generation, and family environment. Children's understanding of media changes as they grow. Each generation experiences and perceives media differently as well.

Millennial children and teens are those who have the high school graduation date of 2000 and beyond. Strauss and Howe (1991) set the dates for the millennial generation as those born in 1982 and later. Millennial children come of age by year 2000 or later and live as adults in the new millennium. Dramatic events the mass media bring to each generation when that generation is coming of age may mark the beginning of that generation's adult consciousness. The events of September 11, 2001, although affecting the consciousness of all Americans, may mark the beginning of and perhaps the nature of the millennial generation's worldview and relationship to the mass media (see chapter 3, "Generations and History"). The media world as it has developed for this millennial generation is a focus of this book.

COMMUNICATION MODELS

The complicated relationship between children and media can be mapped using a communication model. With our focus on a particular audience, the millennial generation, and particular channels of radio, television, and Internet, we now look at the other elements of the communication model. A communication model can represent children's use of media. However, that model has some extra variables we need to consider. The basic communication model includes a source that encodes a message that goes through a channel to a receiver who decodes the message. During the process, noise may interfere with or interrupt the message. After receiving the message, the receiver may provide some feedback for the source (see Fig. 1.1).

For our example, we try to apply the communication model to a 4-year-old watching *Sesame Street* on television (see Fig. 1.2). The source has several layers including public television, the Children's Television Workshop (now called Sesame Workshop), and the producers and characters for the individual show. The encoding process also is multilayered and includes writing the script, taping the show, and preparing the show for satellite transmission. The channel is the satellite, cable system, and television reception the show may go through to reach the child. The channel might also include the videotaping at the home for multiple viewings, the Public Broadcasting Service (PBS) or Noggin (cable channel). The message for programs such as *Sesame Street* is often a prosocial

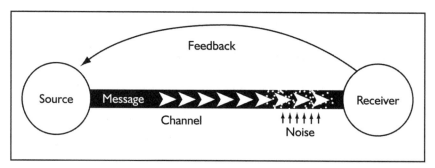

FIG. 1.1.   Communication model.

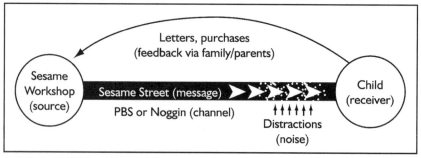

FIG. 1.2.   Child and TV model.

message, such as how to get along and interact with other children. The child, of course, is the receiver, but others may include siblings, parents, or adult caregivers. The child's communication process in this case seems to require an additional variable not included in the general communication model, the mediator between the child and the message, someone who explains or discusses the message with the youth. Thus, the child decodes the message in an environment that may include adult mediation and explanation of the messages. Noise that may interrupt or interfere with a child's understanding of the message includes the physical noise that may occur in the channel or the environment, but can also include the distraction of toys or other youth or adults. In addition, the noise may arise from the child's inability to understand the level at which the message is addressed. Thus the need for an older youth or adult to answer questions has been built into the *Sesame Street* message by having a multiple-level approach in which guests come on, unnamed, who are recognizable to the older youth or adult but not to the 4-year-old child. The celebrity guests make involvement in the communication by older family member more rewarding. Feedback also differs from the standard model in that the older youth or adult may mediate the feedback the child may have to the program. The feedback may be in the form of buying a product such as Tickle Me Elmo or letters from the parent to the public television station about their child's reaction to the show.

THEORETICAL PERSPECTIVES

In addition to mapping the relationship with models, we can try to explain and predict the relationship with theories. A theory tries to explain and predict what will happen in certain circumstances under a given set of assumptions. Theories come from a variety of disciplines including ethics, communication, and psychology. Different theories may also focus on different parts of the communication model, such as the message, the medium, or the receiver. We want to know what causes behavior such as violence, fear, and sexuality. When children in schools behave violently as in the school killings of the late 1990s or imitate the World Trade Center terrorists as one Florida boy did, we want to know what caused that behavior and what we as a society can do to prevent it. We can examine some theories that may help us predict what will happen in the communication process between children and the media.

The theories examine various aspects of the communication model. Some of the theories we examine are macro theories, or theories that examine the larger society. Other theories we examine are micro theories, or theories that examine the individual. Over time, electronic technology has gone from unidirectional broadcast radio and television to the more interactive Internet. The changes in media channel technology parallel the changes in theory that grew to focus more on the receiver and individual use of the media as the 20th century came to a close. As media have become interactive, so have research findings. Some theories focused on the source of the messages and their intent.

Moral Man and Immoral Society by Reinhold Niebuhr

A theoretical overview of the relationship of any individual to society is one place to begin our search for theoretical tools. First we can look at a theoretical perspective that focuses on the source of the message in our communication model. To characterize the media–child–parent relationship, Steyer (2002) referred to media as "The other parent." Thus the source, a societal force, takes the role of parent, an individual source. However, one theory calls society immoral and says the immorality on the societal level conflicts with the moral individual.

The author of *Moral Man and Immoral Society*, Reinhold Niebuhr (1960) took the view that although the individual is a moral and ethical creature, society at large lacks that same dedication to issues of morality: "As individuals, men believe that they ought to love and serve each other and establish justice between each other. As racial, economic and national groups they take for themselves, whatever their power can command" (p. 9).

For the youth's relationship to mass media, this theoretical perspective helps to explain the discrepancy between the socialization the child receives from parents and the differing ethical messages mass media may provide. For example, the family may try to teach youth to resolve problems peacefully. However, media advertisers and producers (sources in the larger society) are interested in the profit they can earn by using violence to attract viewers. The goals of family and society thus differ.

Walsh (1994) used Niebuhr's theory to explain the contradictions we see in the contrast between parent and family messages and television messages:

> Today ... the voice of society contradicts the messages of individual parents. Rather than reinforce them, the larger society undermines and overwhelms the messages of parents, churches, schools, and other agencies designed to help keep our society intact. What is even more alarming is that the voices of our larger society often promote messages which are at odds with the bedrock values of our democratic civilization. (p. 11)

Walsh's "voice of society" may be a difficult one to identify, but it is reflected in part by the economic and political system that Walsh said has profit as its primary motivation. In summary, Walsh said, "The basic disparity comes down to this: what motivates individual parents is ... the desire to 'teach my kids right from wrong.' What motivates our larger, anonymous society is one thing: financial profit" (p. 12). Walsh also seemed to focus on the more negative messages of television found in programs of commercial stations seeking a mass audience. The messages of many public television programs such as *Sesame Street* and children's cable programs such as Nickelodeon's *Blue's Clues* do not seem to contradict what Walsh called "the bedrock values of our democratic civilization" (p. 11). Perhaps their focus exclusively on children allows them to become an exception.

Walsh's (1994) message is similar to Pipher's (1996) message in *The Shelter of Each Other,* in which she argued that it is not possible for parents alone to protect children. The larger society must take on some of the responsibility. In addition, the idea of moral man and immoral society lends itself to a discussion of stereotypes. Individuals may be moral in behavior toward minorities, but how do the mass media act in portraying minorities and women? Are the portrayals immoral?

Niebuhr's (1960) moral man and immoral society theory also reflects in some ways the First Amendment theory of the U.S. Constitution that depended on "moral" individuals to both have free speech and act to correct wrongs if they have the information they need in a free society. However, the First Amendment may at times conflict with protecting children in our society. That protection of children is also a societal value and an exception to some First Amendment protections, as seen in the adoption of the Children's Television Act of 1990 (see chapter 9).

The Medium Is the Message by Marshall McLuhan

Although the source and parental and family mediators are important, the content of the message is also important. The law does not regulate content, because it is crucial to our theory of government to avoid content regulation as provided by the First Amendment. A theory with both macro and micro implications that looks at the channel in the communication model is McLuhan's (1964) "the medium is the message" (p. 7). McLuhan built his perspective on the concept that what the individual gets from the media has little to do with the content of the message, but with the way we get the message and how it affects our senses. McLuhan said that how we receive information changes how we behave and see the world. For example, McLuhan said when the culture's dominant medium is reading, individualism is a strong message. The individualism message the reader gets by reading develops from the reader's strong use of the visual sense alone: Reading is an individual activity in contrast to the oral messages of earlier tribal cultures. McLuhan said print is an extension of the human visual faculty. Just as mechanical technologies extended our hands with hammers and our feet with wheels, print extends the human visual faculty by allowing us to use our eyes to see well beyond our immediate environment to the ideas and visions of people all over the world.

McLuhan (1964) did not address children and the media specifically, but in his analysis of media literacy Meyrowitz (1998) said McLuhan and others offer the concept that regardless of content or production grammar, each medium creates an environment that differs in how both content and production values are organized: "On the micro, single-situation level, medium analyses look at the implications of choosing one medium versus another for a particular communication. Macro, societal-level medium analyses explore how the widespread use of a new medium leads to broad social changes" (p. 105).

In the electronic era, McLuhan (1964) said our culture has begun to extend our nervous system to create a communication system that is making such broad social changes. The electromagnetic spectrum used in radio and television and now in computer technology makes a complete nervous system outside the individual human nervous system. Thus, McLuhan says all previous technologies extended only a particular part of the body. However, the electrical technology is more total and inclusive in how it extends the senses and acts as a nervous system for the society at large. McLuhan's description of the information economy in his 1964 book *Understanding Media* came more than 10 years before the beginning of the information age, that era when information became the product most people were employed to provide: "Under electric technology the entire business of man becomes learning and knowing. In terms of what we still consider 'economy' (the Greek word for a household), this means that all forms of employment become 'paid learning,' and all forms of wealth result from the movement of information" (p. 58). For McLuhan, the medium of electromagnetic communication was the message of a future of "decentralism and diversity" that he imagined as encouraging "self-employment and artistic autonomy" (p. 359).

However, McLuhan (1964) seemed to view decentralization as more idyllic than current concerns for terrorism might provide. Although McLuhan may be considered prophetic, not many theorists have built on these views. One exception is Meyrowitz (1998), who developed an aspect of media literacy he calls "medium literacy" (see chapter 8). Media literacy is a theory in itself that predicts that children who have been trained in how the media work will be better equipped to resist the negative effects of mass media.

Cultivation Analysis by George Gerbner

Concerns with the negative effects of violent and sexual messages are addressed in a theoretical perspective called the cultivation process associated with Gerbner of the Annenberg School of Communication. Since 1967, Gerbner and his colleagues have been researching how television's worldview matches the worldview of heavy viewers of television. As with many of the theoretical perspectives that follow, this perspective is tied to a research technique that focuses on one or more of the elements of the communication model.

Cultivation theory predicts that heavy viewers of television will have different perceptions than light viewers. The research looks at the message through the method called *content analysis* in which the message is studied. In addition, Gerbner and his colleagues use survey research self-reports to determine the perceptions of the receivers, who are evaluated as either heavy or light viewers. The perceptions of heavy viewers are then compared to the perceptions of light viewers. In this way, the researchers try to determine how the aggregate of heavy viewer perceptions of issues such as views against busing may compare to the aggregate content analysis of the messages about race that television may communicate.

> The research consists of two interrelated parts: (1) message system analysis—the annual content analysis of a sample of prime time and weekend- daytime network television dramatic programming and (2) cultivation analysis—determining conceptions of social reality that television viewing may tend to cultivate in different groups of viewers. (Signorielli, Gross, & Morgan, 1982, p. 162)

The different groups of viewers are heavy and light viewers: "Heavy viewers are more likely than are light viewers to hold perspectives and outlooks that are more congruent with television imagery" (p. 170). Thus cultivation theory predicts that people who watch more television will have views of the world that are more similar to television's worldview than other worldviews.

The cultivation process view is a macro view, looking at the whole, rather than the individual.

> Although a viewer's sex, age, or class may make a difference, television helps define what it means, for example, to be an adolescent female member of a given social class. The interaction is a continuous process (as is cultivation) taking place at every stage, from cradle to grave. (Gerbner, Gross, Morgan, & Signorielli, 1986, p. 23)

The content analysis of prime time television is the television worldview Gerbner et al. (1986) used to compare to viewer attitudes: "One lesson viewers derive from heavy exposure to the violence-saturated world of television is that in such a mean and dangerous world, most people 'cannot be trusted' and that most people are 'just looking out for themselves'" (p. 28).

However, that macro view is affected by micro factors such as family environment factors. For example, the mean and dangerous world may cause people to think the world is more violent than it is, but the "expectations of personal victimization depends on the neighborhood of the viewers" (Gerbner et al., 1986, p. 29). As you might expect, for youth and even teens, parental involvement in viewing reduces the cultivation effect, as do strong peer relationships. When everyday experience that is the same as the television world reinforces the views seen on television, the view resonates for the viewer so that, for example, "cultivation of insecurity is most pronounced among those who live in high crime urban areas" (Gerbner et al., 1986, p. 30). This resonance amplifies the cultivation effect. Another characteristic is mainstreaming, which overrides individual differences in heavy viewers such that heavy viewers seem to have very similar perceptions of the world and those perceptions are very similar to the worldview presented in the media. Some of the research on mainstreaming has tried to explain within-group characteristics such as adolescent career choices by looking at the viewing patterns of the individuals in the group (Morgan & Gerbner, 1982).

Some researchers, however, differ with the assumptions of cultivation analysis research. Brown (1993) said cultivation analysis assumes that content is uniform across programming. Another problem with the cultivation analysis approach is the problem of cause and effect. The problem of what came first, the chicken or the egg, could apply to this research, because the behavior of the viewer is seen as the effect when the viewer could be aggressive in nature. Do aggressive children choose to view violent media or does violent media exposure cause children to be aggressive? Correlation is not causation and the relationship between the media and the individual receiver can be very complex (for more, see chapter 5).

Social Learning Theory by Albert Bandura

People tend to believe that children are affected by violence in the media because they observe children imitating what they see in the media. Whereas cultivation analysis focuses partly on the receiver via surveys and groupings of heavy and light viewers, social learning theory looks at the receiver of the message as an individual in a more micro view. Social learning theory is one of the first theories to be applied to the relationship of children to mass media (Van Evra, 1998). Social learning theory and arousal theory predict that children who watch television under certain conditions will learn the behavior they see on television.

Bandura is famous for his BoBo doll experiments, which showed that children will beat up a BoBo doll after watching another person who is rewarded for performing that action. Social learning theory is the explanation Bandura formulated to explain human behavior.

In *Social Learning Theory*, Bandura (1977) presented a four-part process for observational learning (see Fig. 1.3). He began with processes that deal with the attention of the audience. Before individuals can begin to learn, they must be paying attention. Bandura commented on the role of mass media in this process:

> People today can observe and learn diverse styles of conduct within the comfort of their homes through the abundant symbolic modeling provided by the mass media. Models presented in televised form are so effective in capturing attention that viewers learn much of what they see without requiring any special incentives to do so. (p. 25)

Bandura thus characterized the modeling stimuli as distinctive. The arousal level of the viewer is one of many variables that may be used to de-

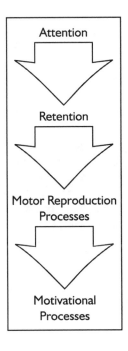

FIG. 1.3.   Bandura's observational learning.

scribe the viewer. For example, a child watches *Sesame Street* each day because the program has characters, such as Cookie Monster, that capture their attention.

Once the modeled event has been attended to, the next step is retentional processes, either in images or words. Repetition is key in the child's ability to retain the images. Words make remembering easier and rehearsal of behaviors also aids in the retention process (Bandura, 1977). Bandura provided some developmental comments for children's retention: "In early years, the child's imitative responses are evoked directly and immediately by models' actions. Later on, imitative responses are usually performed without the models present, long after the behavior has been observed" (p. 27). *Sesame Street* is good at repetition both within the show and across shows. Each show is brought to the viewer by a letter and number. "Brought to you by the number 1 and the letter A," for example.

After the attention and retention, Bandura (1977) called the third step motor reproduction processes; that is, converting symbols into action. Variables in this process include the physical ability to perform the action as well as feedback about the accuracy of the behavior. Children are encouraged to interact and respond while watching *Sesame Street* by singing and talking to the characters that address the children in the home audience.

The last step is the motivational processes; that is, motivation to imitate the original observed behavior. The key to this motivation seems to be observing consequences that reinforce the behavior by reward from others or valuable outcomes for the individual self. Children watching *Sesame Street* may be coviewing with an adult who may reinforce behaviors by praising the child who learns his or her letters and numbers. The show's producers encourage the caregiving adult to coview by including celebrity appearances. The child's self-reinforcement may be the pleasure of learning or simply the pleasure of seeing his or her favorite character. The adult will know if any behaviors are performed when the child yells "Cookie, Cookie" in a voice emulating the Cookie Monster or the child can count to 10 like Count Count.

Other receiver-based theories we examine during the course of this study include schema theory, also called script theory (see chapter 5). Theory not only explains and predicts, but also can inform programmers developing children's programming and help parents and families in deciding what is best for their children. Although theory may help explain or predict media behaviors, it is up to the individual parent or family (see chapter 7) and society (see chapter 9) to provide tools to protect and empower children in their relationship with the mass media.

HISTORICAL OVERVIEW

As theories developed during the various media eras, government and society began to respond to individual constituent concerns with hearings but little legislation for many years. Whereas theory could try to explain and predict, government and society could provide tools for families and children to empower them to control the flow of media messages to their homes. Parents, child advocates, educators, and government representatives have worked to provide these tools. As each medium came into its own, each generation of parents and families worked to provide children with tools to manage the influence of the media as a home utility.

Radio was the first electronic media home utility, but the U.S. Congress passed no legislation for children during the radio era. Parents did complain, however, as early as 1933 when a Scarsdale, New York, parent organization called radio the "Ether Bogeyman" (Cooper, 1996, p. 21). Radio was free and the government charged radio operators to act in the public interest. Because radio was in the home, it was accessible to everyone including children. Because radio was accessible to children more easily than print, children listened to "adult" radio including *The Shadow,* as well as children's programs such as *Little Orphan Annie* (for more see chapter 3).

Television is the first mass medium to have federal legislation for children's benefit, which now limits the number of minutes of commercials on children's television. Parent and family advocacy groups such as Action for Children's Television (ACT) headed by Peggy Charren worked for 20 years to get the Children's Television Act (CTA) into law. The CTA and supporting Federal Communications Commission (FCC) regulations provide parents, families, and caregivers Internet access to local broadcasters regarding broadcast educational programs and limits on advertising for children's programs. In addition, the Telecommunications Act of 1996 required both television manufacturers and cable operators to provide the V-chip to help parents and families to block programming they consider inappropriate for children.

The Internet effectively has combined various mass media in a process known as *convergence.* The various mass media of print, broadcast audio, and video have come together on the World Wide Web. Perhaps most successful (although also subject to court reviews) has been the Children's Online Privacy Protection Act (COPPA, 1998) that seeks to require that parents give their permission for information Web page operators solicit from children. Congress made COPPA law and there have been no First Amendment challenges. The Federal Trade Commission supported this act with regulations that supported children's right to privacy and parents' right to have Web operators get their permission for using information gathered from their children (Kidz Privacy, 2002). Commercial vendors also have provided parents with tools to prevent children from accessing Internet sites that parents can block with filtering software (see chapter 9).

In addition to Internet access to local broadcasters regarding broadcast educational programs, limits on advertising for children's programs, the V-chip, and required parental permission for Internet providers gathering information about children, schools are using media literacy to empower children to both use and analyze mass media. Media literacy as a theory combines the theoretical with the practical. Theoretically, media literacy assumes that children can be empowered both to use media to their advantage and that power by the individual also protects the child from negative effects (see chapter 8).

SUMMARY

We began with our own experiences with the mass media when we were children to ground us in our personal relationship to the mass media. To understand our experiences we examine children at various developmental ages and across generations. We look at the variety of effects that can operate due to children's perceptions at different ages including fear, aggression, and sexuality. Theoretical perspectives coupled with research on effects explain and predict how the communication process may occur. Cultivation theorists, for example, look at the message with their yearly content analysis of prime time and they also look at the receivers or audience as they examine self-report surveys to compare light viewers with heavy viewers. Concerned families and child advocates have worked to empower individuals in their use of television and the Internet through legislation such as the CTA of 1990 and COPPA. The schools also have a role through the teaching of media literacy.

FOR FURTHER CONSIDERATION

1. Using the excerpt from Wally Lamb's *She's Come Undone* as a model, write your own brief description of an encounter you had with a mass medium as a child.
2. Take some time to develop your own communication model for children by using the variables listed in this chapter. Label the variables, but draw it so

that the viewer can understand your model without reading it. Be sure to use an example with a child.

3. Choose an example that shows the relationship of children and the media and then choose one of the theoretical perspectives you think best explains or predicts your example.
4. Choose one of the mass media and explain how its history may help explain the relationship of children and the media.
5. Research the function of the FCC, Federal Trade Commission (FTC), or Congress in establishing policy for children and the media. Be ready to explain your findings in class.

RESOURCES ON THE WEB

The following Internet sources have additional information on the topics in this chapter: the first two are children's advocacy groups, Center for Media Education and Children Now. The third is the FTC Web site regarding children's privacy. The fourth is the Motion Picture Association of America.

www.cme.org
www.childrennow.org
www.ftc.gov/bcp/online.edcams/kidzprivacy
www.mpaa.org/movieratings

REFERENCES

Bandura, A. (1977). Social learning theory. Englewood Cliffs, NJ: Prentice-Hall.
Brown, J. D. (1993). Theoretical view. In B. S. Greenberg, J. D. Brown, & N. Buerkel- Rothfuss (Eds.), Media, sex and the adolescent (pp. 19–25). Cresskill, NJ: Hampton.
Cooper, C. (1996). Violence on television, Congressional inquiry, public criticism and industry response: A policy analysis. New York: University Press of America.
Dennis, E. E., & Pease, E. C. (Eds.). (1996). Children and the media. New Brunswick, NJ: Transaction.
Gerbner, G., Gross, L., Morgan, M., & Signorielli, N. (1986). Living with television: The dynamics of the cultivation process. In J. Bryant & D. Zillmann (Eds.), Perspectives on media effects (pp. 17–40). Hillsdale, NJ: Lawrence Erlbaum Associates
Kidz Privacy. (2001, January 24). Federal Trade Commission Web page. Retrieved June 4, 2002, from www.ftc.gov/bcp/online.edcams/kidzprivacy/
Lamb, W. (1992). She's come undone. New York: Washington Square Press.
McLuhan, M. (1964). Understanding media: The extensions of man. New York: McGraw-Hill.
Meyrowitz, J. (1998). Multiple media literacies. Journal of Communication, 48, 96–108.
Morgan, M. J., & Gerbner, G. (1982). TV professions. In M. Schwartz (Ed.), TV & teens, experts look at the issues: Action for Children's Television (pp. 121–127). Reading, MA: Addison-Wesley.
Niebuhr, R. (1960). Moral man and immoral society: A study in ethics and politics. New York: Scribner's.

Pipher, M. (1996). *The shelter of each other: Rebuilding our families.* New York: Ballantine.

Signorielli, N., Gross, L., & Morgan, M. (1982). Violence in television programs: Ten years later. In D. Pearl, L. Bouthilet, & J. Lazar (Eds.), *Television and behavior: Ten years of scientific progress and implications for the eighties* (Vol. II, pp. 158–173). Washington, DC: U.S. Department of Health and Human Services and National Institute of Mental Health.

Steyer, J. P. (2002). *The other parent: The inside story of the media's effect on our children.* New York: Attria Books.

Strauss, W., & Howe, N. (1991). *Generations: The history of America's future, 1584 to 2069.* New York: Quill.

Van Evra, J. (1998). *Television and child development* (2nd ed.). Mahwah, NJ: Lawrence Erlbaum Associates.

Walsh, D. (1994). *Selling out America's children.* Minneapolis, MN: Deaconess.

The Developing Child and Teen

A CHILD'S PERCEPTIONS

As we know from our own experiences, children and even teens have different perceptions of mass media and use media differently than adults. The changes a child goes through in growing up are the same for children at certain ages. For example, all preschool-age children have characteristics in common based on their lack of experience with the media. At first, like Dolores who began this book, preschoolers tend to learn by stereotyping as Dolores did in her recollection of the delivery men as Presidents Nixon and Eisenhower. Like Dolores, preschoolers have little experience with life, including mass media, and may be frightened or confused in trying to discern what is real. We can view the mass media theory we examined in chapter 1 such as social learning theory (Bandura, 1977) with the variable of the child at different ages: "(Children) are seeing, and trying to interpret the adult world through children's eyes and with children's cognitive capacities" (Van Evra, 1998, p. 45). Not only do child and teen perceptions differ from adult perceptions, but they differ by developmental age as well.

Jaglom and Gardner (1981) compared a child's first encounter with television to that of an anthropologist exploring a different culture:

> As a naive viewer of television, the young child is faced with a formidable task—one reminiscent of the challenge confronted by an anthropologist visiting an exotic land. Like the anthropologist, the child beholds a novel, confusing world that she must attempt to unravel—in this case, the televised world of flickering images and sounds. With relatively little help from informants, he or she must examine these messages, classify them, and establish a meaningful organization. Moreover, young children must devise ways of relating their own experiences to the world contained within a box and separated by a glass screen. In the course of these "ethnographic" explorations, they must learn to make distinctions as well as to draw connections among various programs and characters. Children also must discover the rules that govern the world of television. Only such knowledge will permit prediction of

when a show will begin or end, when a character will appear or disappear, when a program will invade their own world, and when it will transport them into the realm of fantasy and adventure. (pp. 9–10)

The "world contained within a box and separated by a glass screen" is the world of television and the Internet. Children cannot enter the box, but they spend a lot of time in front of it and have differing perceptions of the meaning of what they observe. Those perceptions differ both due to their ability to understand cognitively and their ability to make sense of the reality or fantasy of the message. Doubleday and Droege (1993) saw the child-anthropologist as investigating the mass media with both cognitive processes and sense-making activities.

COGNITIVE PROCESSES

As with social learning theory we investigated in chapter 1, the first cognitive process that must be engaged is attention. If the mass medium does not have the attention of the child or teen, it will not be effective. In the United States, attention is critical for the advertiser, who is paying for the audience's attention to support the programming. For children, attention is determined at least in part by age because ability to comprehend is at least in part tied to age. As children's comprehension increases, their attention also increases.

Attention and comprehension are interactive in that attention affects comprehension and comprehension also affects attention (Huston & Wright, 1983). The attention differs by gender, with boys being more visually oriented and girls being more auditory in their perceptions. Because boys and girls do not differ in comprehension, the researchers concluded that girls learn through their attention to the auditory information and boys learn the same information by attending to the visual information. Also, violence and animation got boys' attention more than girls' (Alvarez, Huston, Wright, & Kerkman, 1988).

Attention and Formal Features

Formal features aid in maintaining the attention of the viewer. *Formal features* are specific visual and auditory production techniques. Formal features can be visual as with cuts, pans, and zooms or auditory as with types of speech, voice characterizations, sound effects, music, or singing. Formal features also may be program attributes such as action, pace, or variability (Fitch, Huston, & Wright, 1993). Formal features are to audiovisual messages what grammar is to the printed word.

Formal features can be music in a variety of styles used to identify ethnicity (the Spanish word of the day is indicated by Spanish guitar music on *Sesame Street*), historical setting (1950s music for *Happy Days*), geographical area (Western music for the desert), and age (boy bands for middle school or rap for high school). Music as formal feature also includes special effects such as the violin tremolo for intense scary music, a pizzicato for sneaky music, or a glissando on a trombone going down the scale to indicate a character is falling. Other common music special effects are a triangle ding indicating a light bulb going on, a cymbal crash to indicate an idea is out of the bag, and a drum roll to indicate suspense (V. Moore, personal communication, March 11, 2002).

Whether the formal feature is visual, auditory, or a combination, it guides the listener or viewer just as punctuation and other grammar cues lead us through the written word:

> Visual or auditory techniques are used to mark breaks in content, changes in scene, connections between distant events, and as bit and program boundary organizers. They are analogous to punctuation, capitalization, paragraphing, and chapter headings in print. We call this the segmental marker function of formal features. (Huston & Wright, 1983, p. 46)

Formal features intend to guide the listener, and they succeed in varying degrees. Huston and Wright (1983) reported on several formal feature patterns. They found "nonverbal auditory features such as lively or loud music, sound effects, peculiar voices, nonspeech vocalizations, and auditory changes recruit and maintain children's attention" (p. 42). Some visual features such as special effects and pans maintain attention, but zooms lose attention. Both moderate and rapid action can hold attention, but moderate action is more effective at communicating information about the plot, whereas rapid action is effective only as sensory stimulation. Physical action, not violence, is associated more with preschoolers' attention.

Comprehension and Children's Characteristics

The second cognitive process following attention is comprehension. What do children comprehend when they do pay attention? Age is an important variable in comprehension. Older children understand formal features more readily than younger children do: "Studies suggest that older children detect the subtle feature cues marking transitions more readily than younger children do and that their attention patterns are more consistently guided by such transitions" (Huston & Wright, 1983, p. 47). Preschoolers and children up to age 7 or 8 do not retain much central content. They recall only isolated events and do not focus on plot. Hence, successful programs for this age group include formats that have isolated events such as *Sesame Street*'s magazine format of animation, Muppets, and human activities. Although *Sesame Street* has a loose structure, more depends on character identification and isolated events and information rather than plot.

In addition to age, the child's skill with program complexity is a factor in comprehension. Program complexity is demonstrated in part by the medium's formal features (Fitch et al., 1993). How children use the formal features depends on their knowledge, which then guides how they understand the message. Collins (1981) listed three forms of knowledge necessary for understanding programs:

> (1) Knowledge of common formats for exposition (for example, narratives, commercial appeals); (2) general knowledge of, and expectations about, situations and event sequences (that is, how events and interactions ordinarily proceed), commonly referred to as world knowledge; and (3) knowledge of the form and conventions of the television medium. These three types of knowledge have been characterized as *schemata*, relatively abstract representations of common phenomena that guide the processing of new instances. (p. 34)

Formal features on *Sesame Street,* for example, include musical themes ("Can you tell me how to get to Sesame Street?"), recurrent formats ("brought to you by the letter A"), and camera transitions such as fades, dissolves, and wipes. Doubleday and Droege (1993) said these formal features "seem to function as an aid in children's selection of content to process and thereby also an aid in comprehension" (p. 27).

To age and skill in program complexity Doubleday and Droege (1993) added experience limitations to the variables that affect comprehension. Younger children's more limited experience leads to poor comprehension by some and more close attention to familiar content. In looking at measures of comprehension and recall, Clifford, Gunter, and McAleer (1995) found that general knowledge is a better predicting variable than age: "Thus it appears that it is not accumulated years (age), but rather accumulated knowledge and possibly developed information-processing skills that predict the amount of novel learning that will take place upon viewing a factual television program" (pp. 211–212). They determined no effect by gender or language ability. Clifford et al. (1995) looked at learning from science programs. They found that:

> Level of relevant background general knowledge emerged as a key variable in relation to learning from science programs. This factor swamped all other demographic, reading, and viewing factors in predicting or explaining variance in recall and comprehension performance. This factor, more than any other, testifies to the fact that what a child takes away from a viewed program depend [sic] critically on what he brings to it. (p. 215)

As children gain experience in their environments, their perceptions become more sophisticated. As they get older, they gain skill in understanding program complexity. These factors lead to greater comprehension as children grow up and experience life and mass media messages.

SENSE-MAKING ACTIVITIES: WHAT IS REAL?

In addition to cognitive processes, sense-making activities are an important set of variables to children's developmental use of media. Just as children learn to "read" the alphabet and numbers, they also "read" formal features. They learn that a black screen is a break from one idea or topic to the next. Formal features are not about content but about form, just as McLuhan theorized in his the medium is the message we examined in chapter 1 (Huston & Wright, 1983). The form of the content communicates the message:

> Forms serve as markers of transitions from program to commercial or from scene to scene, and they act as organizers just as punctuation, spaces between words, and paragraphs organize printed information. Formal features also signal the type of content being transmitted—whether it is fiction or reality, whether it is aimed at children or adults, and the like. They carry connotative meanings about the content. Is it masculine or feminine? Is it violent or nonviolent? Is it fiction or nonfiction? Finally formal features can serve as modes of representing information. The visual and auditory techniques of television are the producer's method of encoding messages. (p. 52)

Children use their experiences to develop their own judgments about reality and even incorporate media depictions into their worldviews. In fact, children's judgments about reality seem to be related to family depictions on television: "Children from 6 to 16 felt that roughly half of all real-life U.S. families are like those in the family series they watch most often.... Television families may be an important source of social learning for children" (Doubleday & Droege, 1993, p. 30).

What do children understand about reality on television? Reality based on cognition is referred to as *factuality*. Looking at factuality, at age 2 to 3, children do not understand the representational nature of television images. By age 4, children have mastered the distinction between real objects and television images. For example, human images are real, whereas cartoons are unreal. News is fact, but entertainment is fiction. Between ages 6 and 11, judgments on factuality increase to the point at about age 10 when they are the same as adult judgments. Reality based on motives for viewing and television experience is referred to as *social realism*.

What cues do children use to judge reality? Both reality and genre of the program can be determined by examining formal features (see *"Challenger Disaster,"* chapter 4). For a younger child, the physically impossible identifies fiction, but for older children, formal features provide the cues (Fitch et al., 1993). Reality is an important variable because it determines credibility. Are children more influenced by television if they think it is real? Yes, and the effect can be seen that "perceived reality ... influenced ... real-world beliefs, particularly for older children" (Fitch et al., 1993, p. 46).

A critical area for children to make sense of content is in the advertising, where children are not only being informed but persuaded to choose a product. Thus distinguishing program and commercial content is an area of concern and research. Again, age is a major variable in children's cognitive processing of commercials, with younger children being more affected by the persuasive messages than older children. Although children between 7 and 9 years of age may understand that the intent of the commercial is to persuade them to buy a product, children that age do not understand the techniques used by the advertisers until they are teens: "By adolescence children have at their disposal more of the cognitive tools necessary to help them distinguish program and commercial content, evaluate commercial messages, and take charge of the influence commercials will have on their consumer behavior" (Doubleday & Droege, 1993, pp. 31–32).

FANTASY, IMAGINATION, AND CREATIVITY

Greenfield et al. (1993) defined imagination as "any form of representational activity that creates entities or events not found in the present or immediately preceding stimulus situation" (p. 58). In their study on program-length commercials, Greenfield et al. also cited research that examines children's responses to viewing by playing with toys related to the program viewed to show creativity: "Television, particularly when combined with thematically related toys, functions as a cultural tool that aids the imaginative development of younger children" (p. 67). However, the factors seem to change when the child is in second grade or older when the use of the related toy means less creativity. Greenfield et al. concluded, "television and program-related toys change the source of imagination, rather than its creativity or quantity" (p. 69).

Singer (1993) found children who watch less television are more creative. Singer identified two criteria for creativity: originality and meaningfulness to others. Singer noted that "ability to search for visual details ... was enhanced in children who spent less time watching television" (p. 78). Singer added, "The more young children viewed, the more similar their real-life stories were to television" (p. 79). Thus, their stories were deemed more original if they were not like television. However, Singer found educational programming for young children can lead to creativity due to its slower pace and the interaction of the audio and video modes.

Singer (1993) also looked at mass media separately. Radio seems to stimulate more creativity and verbal content. Television stimulates more action on the part of the viewer. Singer saw real potential for active responses by the viewer. Thus, interactive media such as the Internet have potential for informative communication. Interactive technologies can motivate children to explore more in problem solving and to achieve more.

MEDIA PERCEPTUAL CHARACTERISTICS BY AGE

Children at various ages in their development use the mass media differently. A specific program illustrates each age of development. The programs have been constructed to take advantage of the characteristics of the stage of development of their intended audiences.

Preschoolers 2–5

> *Preschoolers perceive isolated events and retain stereotypical information.*

As in Wally Lamb's description in *She's Come Undone* (see chapter 1), preschoolers "recall isolated events rather than plots and prefer magazine formats to plotted programs" (Doubleday & Droege, 1993, p. 32). Their retention is more stereotypical, and when they make recognition errors, those errors are more stereotypical. One undergraduate told the class about her preschool perception of an African American adopted cousin as a television show star because both her cousin and the television star were Black children in White families. Dolores, the character in *She's Come Undone*, also is inclined toward stereotypical recognition errors by recalling that the television delivery men were Presidents Nixon and Eisenhower. Programs such as *Sesame Street* use that stereotypicality with such characters as Cookie Monster and Count Count both to guarantee character recognition and communicate their information.

Preschoolers are in the process of learning that television programming is not real. By 4 or 5, children can differentiate the ads from the programs. Although preschoolers trust commercials more and are more affected by what we have called formal features than older children, they recall and understand the commercials less than older children (Doubleday & Droege, 1993). The vulnerability of preschoolers has been addressed in advertising directed at children when advertisers were required to show toys only with the actually propelling mechanism rather than an animated version of what the toy can do.

Younger Children 6–8

> *Younger children learn best when audio and video are interdependent, as with reading to children and the use of a narrator in plays and on television. Younger children have begun to understand plots and benefit from intertextuality, the same storyline in a variety of media.*

As children move into school, their attention to mass media grows. One distinguishing characteristic of younger children, ages 6 to 8, is the development of the relationship of the audio and visual senses. Because of this development, a narrator plays an important role here. A child of this age does better in both attention and comprehension if the narration tells the child the story while he or she watches it. Although central content still is not comprehended and retained much at this age, younger children like plots and can recall content better than preschoolers. Like preschoolers, children ages 6 to 8 are influenced by formal features. Younger children still have higher trust but lower recall and understanding of commercial messages. However, they begin to understand the persuasive intent of advertising (Doubleday & Droege, 1993).

The Magic School Bus is an example of a program that is both popular with 6- to 8-year-olds and is keyed to the developmental level of younger children. The Magic School Bus is both a book series and television program, thus adding the advantage of *intertextuality* by which the child is exposed to the story in books and television, increasing familiarity with the characters and stories. The Magic School Bus television show began on PBS but then went to Fox Kids' Network television. The story is narrated by one of the students in Ms. Frizzle's class. The formal features are the animation of the trips of the school bus into the human body, the sea, or any other of the trips the school bus makes in the science lessons of this story and program.

FIG. 2.1.   Children 9 to 12 years old can infer missing content in problem solving shows such as mysteries, a genre Cody MacLellan, age 9, illustrates. Reprinted with permission.

Older Children 9–12

Older children perceive audio and video independently with less stereotypicality so that narration is not needed and characters can be seen as individuals. Older children recall content in plots and can infer missing content. Older children can solve problems in a variety of contexts, from mysteries to game shows.

Older children are in their middle elementary years, ages 9 to 12. At this developmental stage, children can process audio and video independently so that narration is not necessary. As early as age 8, children begin to do a much better job at recalling central content and inferring missing content and relations between scenes. For that reason PBS television programs such as *Shelby Woo, Ghost Writer,* or *The Wild Thornberries* are on target for this age group. In these programs, the viewer can follow along and solve the problems with Shelby or the Ghost Writer team or the Thornberry family. Older children also retain less stereotypical information. Ensemble casts of diverse ethnic and ability backgrounds work well here. Older children are better able to differentiate programs from commercials and both recall and understand the commercial messages. In addition, older children pay less attention to commercials and they trust the messages less. Older children are more critical and less affected by formal features (Doubleday & Droege, 1993).

Younger Teens 13–15

The television view of the world is similar to the teen view of the world: Consequences are not important to teens or to television. Violence learned at a younger age may manifest in the younger teen and violent tendencies may also turn inward in depression and suicide.

Perhaps it seems that by age 13, the media influence may be less. However, teens are at risk in several areas. They are not adults, nor are they children. They are in the developmental stage we call adolescence. Teens rank the media close to peers as an important source of information. In some studies teens rank parents first. Strasburger (1995) characterized television as a "super peer group" (p. 13) for teens. Although teens look to their peers for information, television can also serve as that nonparental information source. Strasburger characterized the relationship of teens to television in this way: "Teenagers often see themselves egocentrically as actors in their own 'personal fable' in which the normal rules ... are suspended—exactly as on television" (p. 42). The teens are thus a good match for the medium of television in that their view of the world is very similar to television's worldview. In particular, consequences of behaviors are not an important consideration for teens or television. Television does not show and teens do not consider the consequences of violence, sexual activity, or other adolescent behaviors (see Fig. 2.2).

In addition, the aggression teens may have learned at a younger age becomes more evident in their behaviors as adolescents. For example, television violence viewed in third grade correlates with aggressive behavior at age 19 (Strasburger, 1995). (See chapter 5 for more on longitudinal studies and violence.) Although not all teens may

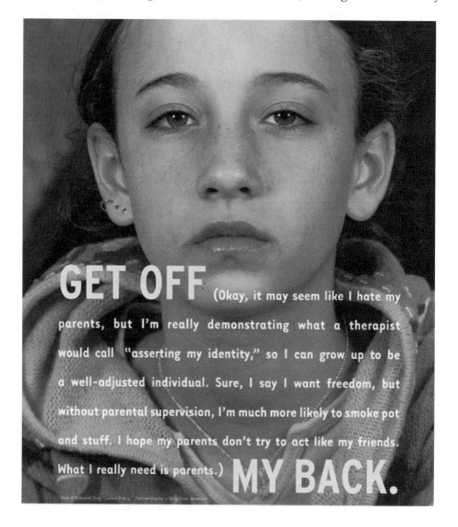

FIG. 2.2. A public service advertisement by the partnership for a Drug-Free America illustrates the characteristics of adolescence as a developmental stage. Reprinted with permission.

show aggression they learned when they were younger, Strasburger (1995) speculated that there is "increased risk of imitative behavior, probably only in certain susceptible teenagers" (p. 35). For example, some teens may be susceptible to aggression turned against themselves, as in suicide. Gould and Shaffer (1986) concluded in their research, "television broadcasts of fictional stories featuring suicidal behavior may in some cases lead to imitative suicidal behavior among teenagers" (p. 693).

Besides their vulnerability based on earlier viewing, Strasburger (1995) said teens are at risk for sexually charged messages: "Although teenagers are probably not as susceptible as young children to media violence, they may be more susceptible to sexual content" (p. 43). Due to their developmental level, teens are searching for nonparental information and television provides an anonymous, entertaining source that serves their information needs. However, the type of information they receive may put them at risk if that information does not best serve their healthy sexual development.

Teens have a very high level of cognitive thinking, but they do not necessarily know how to use that cognition to make decisions. Strasburger (1995) said 70% of teens have their highest level of cognitive thinking by 16, but they do not necessarily have the "'ability to assign priorities and to decide which choice is more or less appropriate than others'" (p. 42), hence problems like a high pregnancy rate. Although teens may know cognitively anything an adult knows, their judgments about sexuality and aggression may be less mature.

Examples of shows for teens are *Sabrina the Teenage Witch* and *Boy Meets World*. In both shows teens make decisions that may not be in their best interests. There still are adults advising these teens. In the case of Sabrina, she has powers that she may not use very judiciously at times. She learns from making mistakes with her magical powers. For Corey in *Boy Meets World,* he also tries out his decision making with real-world results that may hurt his friends, himself, or his family.

Older Teens 16–18

Older teens are developing judgments and their own teen culture.

A secondary level for teen development may be the 15- to 18-year-olds who are developing the judgments that empower their adult cognitive abilities. Examples of channels that target older teens are MTV and VH1, where adults are no longer in advising roles but we see older teens in their own cultural milieu. In the later teen years you also see more independent projects teens do such as the *New Expression* newspaper in Chicago.

NEW EXPRESSION AND YOUTH COMMUNICATION IN CHICAGO

New Expression is a newspaper for high school students in Chicago, distributed to 60,000 teens in 75 public high schools, 25 parochial schools, and 50 park districts eight times a year. Students come to downtown Chicago's Columbia College where the students work on the paper that has as its purpose "to give teens their own voice," according to Youth Communication (YC) Executive Director Bill Brooks (personal communication, 1999). YC is the media organization that publishes *New Expression*. YC is citywide and not just in schools because "kids want bigger issues," Brooks said. Their issues are in their neighborhoods.

For the teen voice to be strong it must be unfettered but also trained, and YC does train the teens. About 150 teens participate in areas including photography and computer-assisted design, as well as reporting and advertising. There are about 15 teen editors and a core of 30 regular reporters. The participants are not chosen but they self-select based on their interests. They learn how to write and express themselves. Their south Loop location in Chicago is easy to access.

YC has a new program in the schools to teach journalism. What is produced in those classes will appear in a special supplement to the regular *New Expression* newspaper. The program is done in 14 high schools biweekly. "N.E. Xtra!" is the lesson-plan package for 800 or more teachers a month who use *New Expression* in their classrooms. YC also does 8-week journalism workshops in their own facilities in the summer taught by Billy Montgomery, who advises *New Expression*. Montgomery is a veteran reporter who has written for the *Chicago Defender* and the *Daily Southtown*. Montgomery also teaches at Columbia College and Roosevelt University. Other cities that have *New Expression*-type newspapers include New York City, Atlanta, Washington, DC, Hartford, San Francisco, and Los Angeles.

The following are accounts of the work of two students with *New Expression* in Chicago, Charles Scott and Dominique Washington.

Charles Scott: Teen Issues at *New Expression* Newspaper

For News Editor Charles Scott, a senior at South Side College Preparatory Academy High School, the neighborhood issues in *New Expression* include the relationship of teens to the Chicago Police Department. After doing a survey on the topic, Scott identified recommendations from teens including "... for police to listen to teens and stop harassing. That was number one. Teens wanted this to change and wanted for the relationship to change," Scott said. And the city stories get reactions from readers and others. A story on the Chicago Transit Authority got 15 letters in response.

Parents and teachers tend to respond to articles about sex. The difficulty of many teen publications has to do with sex as a taboo. Scott said one Chicago high school principal canceled the subscription to *New Expression:* "She said we talked about sex too much. She didn't really read the articles. She just read the headlines. This is what she was talking about, 'Is oral sex all that?'" In the article Marcus Johnson "didn't talk about how to have oral sex. He just talked about, is oral sex all it is cracked up to be?" In addition, a second article on the same page offended the same principal. "She was offended by this whole section on sex," Scott concluded. This entire page is clearly marked with the section heading of "Opinion," Scott said.

The only censorship Scott described was the ability of the principals themselves to keep the newspaper out of their schools. The only other apparent restrictions are those provided by the journalism profession itself. "They can't have any profanity in their writing ... It's in the journalism code," Scott said. "You're not supposed to use profanity period ... You can't talk about a person's race, ethnic group. That's racism."

Dominique Washington: Becoming a Journalist

Dominique Washington, Features Editor, got involved with *New Expression*, a citywide newspaper for teens in Chicago, on a dare. "'I dare you,'" her friend said. "'You talk all this stuff about being a journalist. So I dare you to call.' So I called."

Respect for teens is what *New Expression* tries to develop. Listening to teen voices is one form of respect. "It's time to let youth tell it instead of letting adults tell it," Washington said. "(There's) nothing wrong with letting adults tell it, but wouldn't you like it better from the source if you really wanted to know what was happening with youth in America? Don't let Barbara Walters interview a teen. Let a teen interview a teen. A teen would feel more comfortable."

Threats of violence also are concerns for teens. "One of my journalists just got threatened at school by another student," Washington said. "He did not feel his school handled it fair. He felt that they brushed it off. I found that amazing seeing as though we just got through with this whole killing spree inside our schools that you'd actually take a threat not serious any more. And I said 'Well, you know you have a voice here and you can do it' so they've actually been able to use the newspaper as a voice that they normally wouldn't have."

SUMMARY

Children and teens have different perceptions of mass media that depend on their developmental level, gender, and the characteristics of the source itself including type of media, formal features, and depictions of reality or fiction. Programming can be designed to take advantage of these developmental levels. Children and teens can themselves produce and interact with media in a variety of ways.

FOR FURTHER CONSIDERATION

1. Choose one or more favorite books, videos, or TV programs from your childhood and explain how the medium is structured for the age group you were in when it was your favorite.

2. Find resources in children's or teen media that deal with reality as a topic.
3. Find resources in children's or teen media that deal with imagination or creativity as a topic.
4. Bring to class a recent study that reports a new finding on children or teens and their imagination or creativity as related to mass media.

REFERENCES

Alvarez, M. M., Huston, A. C., Wright, J. C., & Kerkman, D. D. (1988). Gender differences in visual attention to television form and content. *Journal of Applied Developmental Psychology, 9*, 459–475.

Bandura, A. (1977). *Social learning theory.* Englewood Cliffs, NJ: Prentice-Hall.

Clifford, B. R., Gunter, B., & McAleer, J. (1995). *Television and children: Program evaluation, comprehension, and impact.* Hillsdale, NJ: Lawrence Erlbaum Associates.

Collins, W. A. (1981). Schemata for understanding television. In W. Damon (Series Ed.) & H. Kelly & H. Gardner (Vol. Eds.), *New directions for child development: Number 13. Viewing children through television* (pp. 31–43). San Francisco: Jossey-Bass.

Doubleday, C. N., & Droege, K. L. (1993). Cognitive developmental influences on children's understanding of television. In G. L. Berry & J. K. Asamen (Eds.), *Children and television: Images in a changing sociocultural world* (pp. 23–27). Newbury Park, CA: Sage.

Fitch, M., Huston, A. C., & Wright, J. C. (1993). From television forms to genre schemata: Children's perceptions of television reality. In G. L. Berry & J. K. Asamen (Eds.), *Children and television: Images in a changing sociocultural world* (pp. 38–52). Newbury Park, CA: Sage.

Gould, M. S., & Shaffer, D. (1986, September 11). The impact of suicide in television movies: Evidence of imitation. *The New England Journal of Medicine, 314,* 690–694.

Greenfield, P. M., Yut, E., Chung, M., Land, D., Kreider, H., Pantoja, M., et al. (1993). The program-length commercial: A study of the effects of television/toy tie-ins on imaginative play. In G. L. Berry & J. K. Asamen (Eds.), *Children and television: Images in a changing sociocultural world* (pp. 53–72). Newbury Park, CA: Sage.

Huston, A. C., & Wright, J. C. (1983). Children's processing of television: The informative functions of formal features. In J. Bryant & D. R. Anderson (Eds.), *Children's understanding of television, research on attention and comprehension* (pp. 35–68). New York: Academic.

Jaglom, L. M., & Gardner, H. (1981). The preschool television viewer as anthropologist. In W. Damon (Series Ed.) & H. Kelly & H. Gardner (Vol. Eds.), *New directions for child development: Number 13. Viewing children through television* (pp. 9–30). San Francisco: Jossey-Bass.

Singer, D. G. (1993). Creativity of children in a television world. In G. L. Berry & J. K. Asamen (Eds.), *Children and television: Images in a changing sociocultural world* (pp. 73–88). Newbury Park, CA: Sage.

Strasburger, V. C. (1995). *Adolescents and the media, medical and psychological impact.* Thousand Oaks, CA: Sage.

Van Evra, J. (1998). *Television and child development* (2nd ed.). Mahwah, NJ: Lawrence Erlbaum Associates.

CHAPTER THREE

Generations and History

Today's teens want a name that is a founding word, a word that respects their new-ness, a word that resets the clock of secular history around their own timetable. The name *Millennial* acknowledges their technical superiority without defining them too explicitly in those terms. It's a name that hints at what their rising generation could grow up to become—not a lame variation on old Boomer/Xer themes, but a new force of history, a generational colossus far more consequential than most of today's parents and teachers (and, indeed, most kids) dare imagine. (Howe & Strauss, 2000, p. 12)

In addition to the variables of the communication model including sources, messages, channels, and audiences from chapter 1 and the variable of age from chapter 2, we add the variable of generations in this chapter. By viewing the relationship of children, teens and media by generations, we can also examine the history of media during the last 100 years. That media history also is an important variable in the perceptions of children in their relationship to the mass media.

When we think of generations we consider people as a group of the same age, called by social scientists a *cohort*. This cohort group has in common the experi-ences they share because they are born in the same era or time period. Strauss and Howe (1991) in their book *Generations* theorized that each generation has its own characteristics and that four generational profiles go in cycles they traced from the 16th century to the present and into the future. The four types of generations in-clude civic, adaptive, idealist, and reactive. They cited Ortega y Gasset's definition of a generation, "'a species of biological missile hurled into space at a given in-stant, with a certain velocity and direction'" (p. 28).

Strauss and Howe (1991) defined a generation as "a cohort group whose length approximates the span of a phase of life and whose boundaries are fixed by peer personality" (p. 60). They defined peer personality as "a generational persona rec-ognized and determined by (common age location); (2) common beliefs and be-havior; and (3) perceived membership in a common generation" (p. 64).

Williams and Coupland (1997) examined that perceived membership with Generation X in relation to mass media portrayals of their generation. They characterized media as an anchor for the generation: "At some point, all the focus groups defined their generation in terms of media experiences or familiarity with technological advances, as shared by all members of the generation."

The following is presented as a historical essay tracing the history of communication variables for children using generational theory as a framework to look at how each generation has come of age using a different mass media technology. Generational theory states that the characteristic of a generation is forged by the events that occur as the generation comes of age (i.e., becomes adults). Sometimes that coming of age is a dramatic event such as the 1941 bombing of Pearl Harbor, the draft of the Vietnam War, or the events of September 11, 2001. In the modern age, that experience is seen through the filter of the mass media.

THE GI GENERATION AS CIVIC GENERATION

GI stands for government issue, and it refers to what World War II soldiers received as needed for their military service, such as clothing, food, and supplies. The reference to GI later came to identify the generation that served in World War II and received the government issue materials. The radio era corresponded with the GI generation's coming of age. Although radio was not the only medium, as there also were movie newsreels and newspapers, radio was the dominant medium shared by many in the GI generation. Tom Brokaw (1998), in his book *The Greatest Generation*, described a group of people who came of age and developed a generational identity as they came together to fight World War II after Pearl Harbor.

Strauss and Howe (1991) described the GIs (born from 1901–1924) as a civic generation. Civic generations are those who come together to serve the society, often in wartime. If Strauss and Howe were correct about the civic character of the GIs, the GI generation seemed to be helped in reaching that civic-mindedness in part by radio. McLuhan (1964) described the tribal nature of the return to an oral culture that ear-oriented radio encouraged. Radio encouraged the GI children to listen to stories on the radio, just as tribal cultures listen to stories sitting around fires of the hearth. This shift away from the print culture also correlated to the large proportion of immigrant families who were the parents of the GI generation. The immigrant families often were more tribal in that they depended less on print communication and more on oral communication. According to McLuhan, the oral medium by its nature increases the group or societal orientation of the listeners, making them more civic-minded.

At first radio programs were produced locally. Later David Sarnoff of National Broadcasting Company (NBC) and William Paley of Columbia Broadcasting System (CBS) built networks using existing telephone lines. The national radio messages during this era also pulled together the diverse nature of the immigrant populations because the era was one of economic hardships with the Great Depression and then the physical and emotional hardships of war.

Through the era, radio both entertained and informed the youth and adults. For the immigrant parents, there was ethnic radio such as the *Greek Hour* on Chicago radio. For youth and teens, radio introduced them to many of the genres seen now on television. The genres included game shows, Westerns with the *Lone Ranger*, soap operas that originated on radio, adventure programs such as *Captain Midnight*, drama such as *The War of the Worlds* broadcast, and news including the coming war in Europe. The fact that these programs came over the air on only a few national channels meant that the audience members were united in their sources as they had never been before. They needed that quality to go into the throes of World War II.

The message content during the 1920s and 1930s was credible due to the "hearing is believing" aspect and because some important figures mastered the medium. President Franklin D. Roosevelt mastered the medium with his fireside chats. Roosevelt was the first great communicator and he talked children and adults through the fears of the Great Depression. "The only thing we have to fear is fear itself" was the memorable message Roosevelt had for the nation. His voice was recognizable by the radio listeners.

In 1938, the credibility of radio was challenged by *The War of the Worlds* broadcast in which Roosevelt's voice was imitated to contribute to the drama of the invasion by Martians in New Jersey. The genre of the news bulletin interruptions of band music also was familiar and lent to the credibility of the hoax because listeners had been accustomed to news interruptions of band music for European war news.

Comedian Steve Allen told Ellerbee and Gandolph (1986) in an interview for *Our World* about his experience with the *The War of the Worlds* broadcast as a teenager. Allen was living in a hotel in Chicago with his aunts when he heard the news that the Martians were invading. He told Ellerbee that his aunts were panicked and planned to go to Holy Name Cathedral, feeling if they were going to die, they should die in church. However, when they got to the lobby of the hotel, another channel was on with no news of the Martian invasion. Allen said that although he knew little about the final days, he did know it would not be one network's exclusive. Youth who grow up with a medium learn to understand its characteristics and, as they get older, they develop the critical thinking necessary to evaluate its credibility. They often know better than their elders how the medium works.

The Princeton researchers who studied the panic found that critical thinking skills and religious beliefs were two variables that differentiated those who panicked from those who did not. Just as the teenage Steve Allen used his critical thinking to realize that the news bulletin was fiction, 5 million of the 6 million listeners did not panic. Although 1 million people panicked, the 5 million who didn't were using their critical thinking skills to check other channels for comparable news of a Martian invasion, thus avoiding panic. However, just as Allen's aunts panicked and wanted to go to the church, their religious beliefs may have made them more vulnerable to the panic that did affect 1 million listeners.

Television was ready to go in 1939 and NBC showed television at the New York World's Fair. Franklin Roosevelt was the first president to appear on television at the New York World's Fair. However, television's development was held up due to the technology needs of World War II. The technology resources were needed for the war and television was put on hold until the war was over. Radio became the medium of World War II and it allowed listeners to get critical news without seeing the horror of the war. Their support of the war was optimized by this combination of sharing the information without having to see the carnage of the war.

However, it was a GI generation teenager who invented television. Philo Farnsworth, a farm youth, based his invention of electronic television on the idea of farm rows. His electronic version of television scanned the screen to create a frame, just like the film frame that when followed by another frame with slight changes gave the illusion of movement. Farnsworth patented his idea and tried to start his own television company, but the monopoly of radio giant NBC made progress difficult. RCA owned NBC at the time and finally paid for patent use, but the war intervened and Farnsworth's patents lapsed during the war so he lost his ability to capitalize on his ideas. The corporate lifetime outlasted Farnsworth's individual lifetime and his name fell into oblivion until recently, when he received some recognition for his invention, including a statue in the Capitol and documentary films such as *Big Dream, Small Screen* (Trinkl, 1997).

THE SILENT OR BEAT GENERATION AS ADAPTIVE

When World War II ended, the GI generation began to start their own families, but there was another group of children who came of age after the war. Strauss and Howe (1991) called those who were born between 1925 and 1942 the silent generation. Strauss and Howe characterized that generation as adaptive because they were caught between the heroic GIs and the noisy and numerous baby boomers, who by number and character demanded attention. The silent generation came of age amid the Korean War, the McCarthy era of anticommunism, and the rebellion of the beatniks. Often called the beat generation, the silents saw their generation in 1950s plays such as *West Side Story* and films such as *Rebel Without a Cause*. The most visible children's theme was juvenile delinquency, as exemplified by James Dean in *Rebel Without a Cause*. Like the GIs, the early part of this cohort group were radio-oriented with news of the war dominant from the late 1930s on. All the radio stars moved to television when the networks began television right after the war. The television experience of the silent generation included the early unedited television on which comedians such as Milton Berle and Ernie Kovacs could push the envelope of acceptable visual comedy. Walt Disney's *Snow White* set a box office record in 1938 (Strauss & Howe, 1991). Strauss and Howe called the silent generation "America's greatest generation of comedians, psychiatrists and songwriters" (p. 282). However, growing up during war and red baiting also helped to create strong civil libertarians in youth coming of age, as well as younger children and adults:

> The Silent Generation has produced virtually every major figure in the modern civil rights movement—from the Little Rock children to the youths at the Greensboro lunch counter, from Martin Luther King, Jr., to Malcolm X, from Cesar Chavez's farmworkers' union to Russell Means' American Indian Movement. (Strauss & Howe, 1991, p. 285)

Silent generation civil libertarians did what they did in front of the new television cameras and made their points quietly but for all to see. Silents used the new television medium to their advantage to win civil rights for many GIs who had experienced discrimination even as they fought for their country during World War II. Silents were between the heroic GIs and the noisy boomers who outnumbered the silents as they became the focus of the GI generation and later societal attention.

THE BABY BOOMERS AS IDEALISTS

The postwar baby boom allowed a specific beginning to the generation that ranged in birth dates from 1943 to 1960 (Strauss & Howe, 1991). The soldiers came back after 4 years of war and began families to create a baby boom. Television was the dominant medium for boomers, although radio still played an important role, as did newspapers and magazines. An antitrust suit against NBC created a third network with America Broadcasting Company (ABC) in 1943.

The first woman on the FCC, Frieda Hennock, guaranteed the fourth channel for educational television. Thus began the long conflict for claiming children's educational time and space on television that continues today. Early television had some children's shows that live in boomer memories such *as Kukla, Fran and Ollie*, a puppet show seen over WGN (WGN stands for World's Greatest Newspaper and refers to the *Chicago Tribune,* which expanded into radio and television), an independent station in Chicago.

Popular programming for children included the circus-like *Howdy Doody*, Walt Disney's *Mickey Mouse Club*, and *Mr. Wizard*, a science program and precursor to *Bill Nye the Science Guy.* In addition, many of the radio programs came directly to television including *The Lone Ranger,* a Western many children watched. However, the children's programs soon retreated to the cartoon ghetto of Saturday morning. Children watched what adults watched, as many do even today. Some of it was appropriate for children, such as family shows *Ozzie and Harriet* and *Our Miss Brooks.* Comedy lent itself to the visual nature of television with *I Love Lucy,* and situation family comedies like *George Burns and Gracie Allen.*

Some of the television programming was not appropriate for children. There was a lot of violence in the Western genre, science fiction shows such as *Flash Gordon*, and the news. Being able to see the news made it accessible to children in a way that radio did not. Children might tune out the droning of McCarthy hearings, but the visuals of African American children entering a school amid the sneers of others was accessible to even young children. The assassination of John F. Kennedy in 1963, although clearly on tape and not live, was the precursor to the trauma children experienced when the *Challenger* explosion and the death of Christa McAuliffe were on television live. It didn't end there. The weekend JFK died, those who still were watching on Sunday morning could see Jack Ruby assassinate Lee Harvey Oswald live on television. News continued to bring home the assassinations of Martin Luther King, Jr. and Robert F. Kennedy.

Although the Vietnam War had begun in the early 1960s when President Kennedy had sent in advisors, film coverage of the war began later. Several factors worked to make the Vietnam War different from World War II. In addition to Vietnam being an undeclared war, it was filmed without censorship and showed the squalor of war more than the valor. Young people were involved in this war because the U.S. government drafted U.S. teens to become soldiers for a war that was not clearly defined in terms of U.S. self-interests. It was the teens that were drafted and the teens that protested the war that made this war different from World War II.

The boomers came of age during the drafts of the Vietnam War with a choice of whether to fight in Vietnam or to protest that war. During the demonstrations at the 1968 Democratic National Convention in Chicago, young protesters used the slogan "The whole world is watching," showing their self-awareness and their management of the media as they were beaten and tear-gassed by Chicago police. The early protests and marches such as the march on Washington in November 1969 were peaceful and emulated the civil rights protests these youth had witnessed on television as they grew up.

Whether fighting in Vietnam or protesting the war at home, the boomers were idealistic in their strong views of right and wrong and their own ability to set things right, as seen in music:

The first Boomer cohorts came of sexual age with the Beatles' "I Wanna Hold Your Hand," middle cohorts with the Rolling Stones' "Let's Spend the Night Together," late cohorts with Bruce Springsteen's "Dancing in the Dark." Yet whether first-wavers asserting a creative role in an idealized future or last-wavers attempting a more defiant withdrawal from the world, adolescents looked within themselves to find solutions to life's problems. (Strauss & Howe, 1991, p. 308)

Whether in music, film, or television, the media came to the boomers via one-way communication. Any reaction had to be out in the world for their voices to be heard. They could not talk back to their TV sets. Boomers tried to institutionalize that ability to use their voices through technology with the rise of cable television technology and the access movement. Public-access cable television began as a way for citizens to take control of the one-way television messages, a move toward encouraging greater control by the viewer and greater empowerment by being able to use the media to deliver their own messages. When cable television did take off in the late 1970s, the local franchises often included an access requirement for the cable operator to provide the community with equipment, training, and access to cable channels.

Interactive media was a goal for boomers, but the next generation grew up with interactive technology.

GENERATION X AS REACTIVE

For Generation X, born between 1961 and 1981, cable television, videocassette recorders (VCRs), and computers became prevalent. Although cable television had been available since the beginning of television and used in isolated communities, cable television became a way to bring a variety of channels to all homes in the late 1970s, the coming of age of Generation X. The variety of channels also allowed for some channels to specialize in children's programming, such as Nickelodeon in the early 1980s. In addition, the interactivity the boomers sought in public-access cable television became a reality in many communities for the coming of age of Generation X. Beyond that, the interactivity of video and later computer games took off during this time.

The Consumer Electronics Manufacturers Association (CEMA) surveyed adult members of Generation X and found that early exposure to VCRs and video games seems to have carried over to their adult lives:

> CEMA found that video products play an important role in the lives of Gen-Xers. Fifty-four percent agree that video products are a top source of entertainment. Gen-Xers have embraced the concept of home theater; more than half own a TV that measures 27 inches or greater, and one in four owns home theater speakers. ("Digital Technology," 1998, paragraph 4)

Personal computers (PCs) also have made their mark: "The household penetration of PCs for Gen-Xers is 53 percent, as the Internet is becoming a way of life, according to CEMA" ("Digital Technology," 1998).

Gen-X youth reacted to the adult problems around them with few limits on added media exposure. "From the Vietnam hysteria to … Three Mile Island—at every turn, these kids sensed that adults were simply not in control of themselves or the country" (Strauss & Howe, 1991, p. 317). One of the media markers for this generation was the *Challenger* explosion in 1986. Here adults were not in control and children were not protected from the horrors of watching the *Challenger* explode on live television.

While boomers were feeling liberated in their coming of age, the Xers were still children needing the protection of adults:

> An awakening era that seemed euphoric to young adults (boomers) was, to them, (Xers) a nightmare of self-immersed parents, disintegrating homes, schools with conflicting missions, confused leaders, a culture shifting from G to R ratings, new public-health dangers, and a "Me Decade" economy that tipped toward the organized old and away from the voiceless young. (Strauss & Howe, 1991, p. 321)

What the boomers saw as liberation the Xers saw as lack of control. One control Xers were not happy with was the lock on popular culture the Xers sensed the boomers had by their numbers. The images of youth were not very positive. On television young Xers saw

> Max Headroom, beheaded in an accident, imprisoned within TV sound bites; the Teenage Mutant Ninja Turtles, flushed down the toilet as children, deformed by radiation, nurtured on junk food; and Bart Simpson, the "under-achiever" whose creator likens him to everyone's "disgusting little brother"—the "little Spike-Head" (Strauss & Howe, 1991, p. 323)

Other images included the young people in *Breakfast Club* and their cynicism toward the authority of the teacher.

Gen-Xers defined their generation in part by the media they watched. One focus group member for a study on Gen-X generational identity gave this definition:

> 1 Matt: I don't think you can necessarily say that you were born January 1 1976 therefore you are not part of my generation (group laughter) so I don't know maybe it should be more of I don't know if you have watched "Conjunction Junction" as a kid then you are probably part of the generation.
>
> (group laughs)
>
> Matt: (addressing 13, a British woman recently moved to the United States) do you know that song?
>
> 13 no
>
> (Matt starts the "Conjunction Junction" song and other group members join in the song) (group laughs). (Williams & Coupland, 1997)

In addition to "Conjunction Junction" as a media generational identifier, the focus groups suggested *The Brady Bunch* and *Gilligan's Island*.

Like the Michael J. Fox character in *Family Ties,* money is important to this generation: "Money means survival, and for a generation whose earliest life experiences have taught them not to trust others, survival must come first" (Strauss & Howe, 1991, p. 320). With the differing characteristics of boomers and Gen-Xers, management styles have shifted. As Gen-X entered the workforce, their characteristics included needing autonomy in decision making, accepting of constant change, and finding value in differences (Smith, 2000).

Just as Gen-Xers see media programming and content as important to defining their generation (see earlier), they also find the technology they grew up with as an important generational identifier: "Another media identifier appears to be the common generational experience of certain media technology; for example, computer games such as Pac Man and Atari (Focus Group 4)" (Williams & Coupland, 1997).

As a reactive generation, they are socially mature and have good diplomatic skills that take the edge off the idealistic rigidness of the boomers.

GENERATION Y OR MILLENNIALS AS CIVIC

Just as with the last civic generation, the GIs and Pearl Harbor, the millennials' coming of age is marked by a crisis that acted to bring people together to face a common enemy with the events of September 11. The literature now refers to the next and most current generation of children as millennials or Generation Y

FIG. 3.1.   September 11, 2001, in some ways marks the beginning of the Millennial generation. A member of that generation, Matt Tacy, age 10, illustrates the TV images of that event. Reprinted with permission.

(following Generation X). Strauss and Howe (1991) began this generation in 1982, which would have them coming of age in the year 2000 at the earliest. The beginning date, 1982, seems to be based on the high school graduation date of 2000. The coming of age for the oldest members of the cohort group was marked by the events of September 11, 2001.

A Pew Research Center for the People and the Press study in November 2001 found "18- to 25-year olds were more interested in news and had more positive views of government than they did before September 11" (Shearer, 2002, p. 7). The crisis of the events of September 11 seemed to focus the civic generation of the millennials on the news and their government's response to the terrorist threat. The issues millennials are interested in are the issues that affect their lives. Journalists have identified several issues millennials care about:

> Post-secondary education, violence in schools, the quality of high-school educa-
> tion, the environment, poverty and gun control are only a few of the issues that
> young people will read about—that is, if the stories are written to include what
> those topics mean to them specifically. (Shearer, 2002, p. 7)

Young news sources as well as topics they find pertinent complete the profile of this generation for journalists seeking to target the millennial audience.

When Strauss and Howe wrote their description in 1991, they stressed how protective boomers and Xers were of their children: "Grown-up Boomer radicals who once delighted in shocking their own moms and dads now surprise themselves with their own strictly perfectionist approach to child nurture" (p. 338). The protection can also be seen in the legislation that finally was passed in 1990 with the CTA. Protection is accompanied by catering to the children's media programming needs with expanded children's media.

> As the '90s progressed, the Millennials became the most catered-to kids in the history
> of the pop culture. Thanks in part to Congress's new educational-TV rules, Nickel-
> odeon became less an island for a few cable-ready Gen Xers than a generational bond
> for Millennial millions. The Learning Channel, Cartoon Network, and other (mostly)
> kid-friendly networks joined the mushrooming market. By 1999, according to the
> State of Children's Television report, 1,324 kids' programs appeared weekly on 29 chan-
> nels. The top-rated kids' TV shows included Rugrats ..., Teletubbies and The
> Thornberrys. (Howe & Strauss, 2000, p. 250)

Although some protections from media came in the CTA of 1990 in the form of a minimum of educational television hours and a maximum of advertising minutes, the content of much of the media continued to be adult-oriented with violent news involving young people.

With the events of September 11 and school shootings at Columbine and elsewhere, it seems that protection is difficult. Technologically, protection is

difficult, too, with three attempts to restrict indecency on the Internet shot down
due to First Amendment issues in the last 10 years (see chapter 9). Technology is
expanding the millennial world to a more global one:

> If their parents grew up in the confines of cookie-cutter suburbia, these kids are devel-
> oping their interests in a world of exploding technological opportunity, learning
> through computers, video and a bursting array of cable options. This sophisticated,
> mouse-wielding, joystick-operating group grew up with advanced eye-hand coordi-
> nation and a low threshold for boredom. (O'Leary & Rosenthal, 1998, paragraph 23)

Millennials do not know a world without personal computers. They have
interactive media with computers and video games as well as the more extensive
programming on cable and satellite television. The millennials, even more so than
the Xers, are media interactionists, with the Internet being a prime new
technology for this most recent generation.

For some journalists, the nature of the coverage of children in newspapers has
changed with a new beat called the children's beat and a new section called the
Family section.

The Children's Beat and the Family Section

For the millennial generation of children, news values have shifted and
stories about children are on the front page. "There was a real change in
thinking," former *Chicago Sun-Times* children's beat reporter Leslie Baldacci
said. "(The children's beat) is newsworthy where it had not been before. There
was a paradigm shift. It was a radical change. It is on the front page. We hear
now, 'Put it on the front page.'"

In addition to front-page stories about children across the country, The
Chicago Tribune says it provides its readers with the only regular family section
for a newspaper in the United States, Tribune Family Editor Denise Joyce said.
The *Chicago Tribune*'s Family section goes beyond stories of the superachievers
or superabused to cover the full range of subjects of concern to baby boomers
and their millennial generation children.

The Tribune Family section, inaugurated in the Sunday edition in March 1999,
is a features section and part of the national edition of the *Tribune*. *Tribune* staff-
ers, themselves boomers, recognized the need for the section as part of their continuing attempt to "stay in touch with readers," Joyce said. Brainstorming
sessions led them far beyond the standard parent-and-teen stories to articles on
alternative lifestyles, couples, pets, and gay and lesbian families.

"We're trying to branch out," Joyce said. "Trying to do more." The section is
not exclusively about parenting or addressed to women. They have focused on
fathering roles. "We have a healthy share of male readership," Joyce said.

Family section stories are the ones people talk about in the bleachers of
children's sports games, Joyce said. How much TV should kids watch? How do

you know if your child is doing drugs? The audience is the parent as part of the family, not the children, although some teens and college-age children might also read stories about public versus private colleges or stories about senioritis.

The children's beat did not last at the *Chicago Sun-Times*. "1990 to 1993 was an experiment," Baldacci said (see other boxed story for history). "Others picked up pieces of it." Today there is a RealLife section of The *Sun-Times* done by Susan Dodge that includes related issues such as feature stories ranging from stories on schools to coed sleepovers. The *Sun-Times* also has a family page on Sunday with news briefs and stories such as those about gays raising children.

The future of the family page at The *Chicago Tribune* will depend on its ability to pay for itself. If you ask what role readers play as opposed to what role the bottom line plays in deciding to maintain a section, the answer is "It's both," Joyce said. You have to be fiscally responsible. Sections like the family section have to pay for themselves, Joyce said. Today's readers do not have the same interests as those in the 1950s and 1960s. What would hit home? There is a huge interest in family issues now.

The Development of the Children's Beat in Newspapers of the 1990s

The development of a family section for a major metropolitan newspaper was the culmination of many developments in the 1990s. The *Tribune's* only major Chicago competitor is the *Chicago Sun-Times*. The *Sun-Times* tried a children's beat in the early 1990s. Former *Chicago Sun-Times* children's beat reporter Leslie Baldacci was the primary reporter. At the *Sun-Times,* the beat Baldacci reported on started out as a beat on parenting. She says they did fun stuff, such as product trends, but sometimes pointed out the harm being done when the fun was at the expense of the children. In the "diaper derby," held in the middle of Chicago Bulls games, infants crawled to a finish line. However, said Baldacci, the problem with the "diaper derby" was that it was held in the loudest stadium in the country, Chicago Stadium, and the children were awake well past their bedtimes.

As the 1990s progressed, so did Baldacci's beat. Due to events in Illinois at that time, the beat began to focus on social welfare. "We found ourselves in a crisis on child welfare," she said. The number of children in state care doubled. The "parenting" beat became a "social welfare" beat. The question "What is good parenting?" evolved into descriptions of children dying and examples of bad parenting. The beat changed again when Baldacci spent a lot of time in juvenile court. "It morphed into a juvenile justice beat," she said. There was a rise in juvenile crime, and children were killing other children. Again the beat changed. This time Baldacci worked a police and court beat with a social pathology bent.

Baldacci fought for the more positive stories, but journalism values immediacy and features breaking news. Early in the process of children's beats, the journalists played off breaking news. However, reporters, especially women, also developed stories based on their own parenting. "I come from a very hard news background," Casey Journalism Center Director Beth Frerking said. "I cover floods and fires and hurricanes and politics and plane crashes and all that kind of stuff which I loved. I enjoyed doing all that.... I get very annoyed at the sort of dismissiveness of some editors about children. 'That's just kids.' Well that's people's lives. It's as important as what's going on in Chechnya or wherever."

Frerking calls the stories she began doing in the early 1990s bus stop stories. "I wrote about my life," Frerking said. "I found that those stories almost across the board always played best. I did a lot of trend stories. I didn't do as much reporting on disadvantaged children, because that tends to be a more local story.... I did a huge thing on foster care, but not the classic kids burned with cigarettes. I did a piece on the everyday obstacles foster kids face in the system and how it wears them down, not the huge tragic things, but the little things that add up."

Perhaps like the GIs who learned how to face adversity through the Depression, the problems millennials see in the schools will help them to pull together even more as a civic-minded generation to face an internal or external enemy. The events of September 11, 2001 marked the coming of age of the millennials just as Pearl Harbor did for the GIs. Some speculate the next group will be Generation Z (born 2001–2020; Howe & Strauss 2000) and get their name as their character develops.

SUMMARY

You may disagree with the theory and Strauss and Howe's (1991) premise about generations having characteristics that run in cycles. However, the generational theory they presented gives us a context for looking at the relationship between the audience and the communication media in various eras. The thesis that emerges is that each generation comes of age with its own new communication medium and they are its masters. However, as McLuhan (1964) said, the medium itself also is the message and molds how the people who use it think and perceive the messages they receive. The dominant communication medium also may affect the approach of the audience to communication and problem solving. We as human beings have created a digital nervous system for our society much like the nervous systems we have as individuals. The communication system has grown from one-way mass communication to interactive and very individual communication. For children, each communication technology has problems shared by all the others and new problems unique to that medium.

FOR FURTHER CONSIDERATION

1. Identify yourself by generation and write a historical essay using your recollection of events, especially media events, that may have shaped your generational identity. Do you agree with Strauss and Howe? Does each generation have an identity?
2. Prepare a detailed model (perhaps the one you developed earlier) to show the interaction of the generational variables detailed earlier: source, channel, audience, noise, message, and feedback.
3. Conduct focus groups as Williams and Coupland (1997) did to determine Gen-X or millennial concepts of their own generation. Here are some of their questions:
   a. "How do you think the media portrays your generation?"
   b. "Do you think this is an accurate portrayal?"
   c. "Do you think they (parents) have a good view of what your generation is or what you're about?"
   d. "What do you think other generations are saying about your generation?"
   e. "How would you describe yourself? … Why?"
   f. "How would you describe your generation?"

REFERENCES

Brokaw, T. (1998). *The greatest generation*. New York: Random House.
Digital technology sparks Generation X. (1998, September 22). *Electronic News, 44* [Electronic version]. Retrieved February 22, 2002, from EBSCOhost.
Ellerbee, L., & Gandolph, R. (Writers). (1986). Our World 1938 (Television series episode). In *Our World*, an ABC production on *War of the Worlds*. New York: ABC.
Howe, N., & Strauss, W. (2000). *Millennials rising: The next generation*. New York: Vintage Books.
McLuhan, M. (1964). *Understanding media: The extensions of man*. New York: McGraw-Hill.
O'Leary, N., & Rosenthal, N. (1998, May 18). The boom tube. *Adweek Eastern Edition, 39*, 20. Retrieved June 24, 2002 from EBSCOhost.
Shearer, E. (2002, April). Generation ignored. *American Journalism Review, 24*, 7.
Smith, B. (2000, November). Managing Generation X. *USA Today Magazine, 129* [Electronic version]. Retrieved February 22, 2002, from EBSCOhost.
Strauss, W., & Howe, N. (1991). *Generations: The history of America's future, 1584 to 2069*. New York: Quill.
Trinkl, A. (Producer). (1997). Big dream, small screen. A Windfalls Film for *the American Experience* with David McCullough. Boston: WGBH Educational Foundation.
Williams, A., & Coupland, J. (1997, September). Talking about Generation X: Defining them as they define themselves [Electronic version]. *Journal of Language and Social Psychology, 16*. Retrieved June 25, 2002, from EBSCOhost.

PART II

Audience Reactions

Perceptions of Fantasy and Reality

"What is REAL?" asked the Rabbit one day, when they were lying side by side near the nursery fender, before Nana came to tidy the room. "Does it mean having things that buzz inside you and a stick-out handle?"

"Real isn't how you are made," said the Skin Horse. "It's a thing that happens to you. When a child loves you for a long, long time, not just to play with, but REALLY loves you, then you become REAL." (Williams, 1958, pp. 16–17)

WHAT IS REAL?

Several generations of children have enjoyed the theme of *The Velveteen Rabbit, Or How Toys Become Real*. The theme of toys becoming real is prevalent in literature and electronic media. For children, what is real may not be something external to the child's life, but something that is part of the internal development of that child. In her book *Fake, Fact, and Fantasy*, Davies (1997) said the important element is whether the story is authentic to the child:

> What would matter most for children when they try to judge representations of the real world, whether on television or anywhere else, is not how literally true to life these representations are, but how authentic they are perceived to be in addressing children's own concerns and preoccupations. This functional definition of *real* can also be helpful for parents: Realistic representations are accounts of human experience that they find useful in explaining how the world works to their children. Parents and other adults have always used a variety of myths and stories in carrying out their task of socializing the next generation. By this definition, *The Wizard of Oz* may very well seem to be more real—that is, personally useful—to young children than the news. (p. 22)

If the story is useful in explaining how the world works, it is real. Davies grounded her research in children's own definitions of reality. Her respect for children's

FIG. 4.1.   Calvin and Hobbes consider if life should be more like TV. CALVIN AND HOBBES © Watterson. Reprinted with permission of UNIVERSAL PRESS SYNDICATE. All rights reserved.

perceptions is based on her view that because children do not conform to adult views, they hold hope for the development of the human race. Generation theory (see chapter 3) also supports the view that children's innovations are critical for each generation of youth as they strive to continue to improve society.

> Children's tendency to resist adult-imposed ideologies and behaviors through their private rituals, games, fantasies, tastes, and interpretations of reality both in life and in art, is a developmentally desirable one, and it has the evolutionary survival value of making sure that human diversity and adaptability continue. Children's abiding preoccupation with alternative realities—with pretend games—almost from birth, suggests an extreme unwillingness to accept untested, adult versions of what life is supposed to be about. To put it more bluntly, kids are hard to brainwash. (Davies, 1997, p. 146)

Although children's resistance to adult views may be an opportunity to put their own mark on the world, to make that mark they will use the media instruments of their cohort group as well as earlier and later technologies to develop the messages of their generation. Like any view that focuses on the audience and what they do with the message, looking at what children do with the messages they develop is critical to understanding the process.

In this chapter we examine children's perceptions of messages and how they may discern fact from fiction. Effects tied to the issue of fantasy and reality for children may include fear, grief, and trauma. In addition, there is some research on how some television programming may affect children's fantasy life by increasing or decreasing imaginative play with toys related to programming. We examine how children may determine program content from persuasive messages and what they do with toys related to programming.

DEVELOPMENTAL STAGES AND FEAR

For children, stimuli for their imaginings are as important to them as food and milk is for the development of their bodies. The message sources may be parents, peers or electronic media. The concern for the messages in the area of reality perceptions has to do with the role of fear. You may remember what frightened you as you were growing up. Perhaps you were comforted with the words "It isn't real." However, especially for younger children, those words are not comforting. As in many effects variables, the age of the child is the best predictor of the child's fright response. Although it is not true that the child simply becomes less and less susceptible to fright, children are frightened of different things at different stages of development (Cantor, 1996):

> Children from approximately 3 to 8 years of age are frightened primarily by animals; the dark; supernatural beings, such as ghosts, monsters, and witches; and by anything that looks strange or moves suddenly. The fears of 9–12-year-olds are more

often related to personal injury and physical destruction and the injury and death of relatives. Adolescents continue to fear personal injury and physical destruction, but school fears and social fears arise at this age, as do fears regarding political, economic, and global issues. (pp. 95–96)

Thus for small children, animals and monsters are sources of fear (see Fig. 4.2), but as the child gets older, those fears from fantastic media depictions subside and fears of personal harm from kidnapping, accidents, and natural disasters are more prevalent (see Fig. 4.3). The fears become more abstract as the child grows until the fears focus on school exams, dating, and even war (Cantor, 1996).

CHILDREN'S RESPONSES TO MAJOR NEWS EVENTS

The point is that children do react to media messages based on their developmental stage and those reactions are different from adult reactions. In each generation, there are media news events that mark that generation's memory. For GIs it was Pearl Harbor and for boomers it was the Kennedy assassination and the Vietnam War. We examine events that marked Gen-X and millennials. For Gen-X it is the *Challenger* disaster and the Gulf War; for millennials it is the events of September 11, 2001.

FIG. 4.2. Children's fears vary by age. Devin Donohue, age 11, illustrates fear of animals especially typical of children 3 to 8 years old. Reprinted with permission.

Challenger Disaster

Many children learned of the deaths of the *Challenger* astronauts, including teacher Christa McAuliffe, when at school and some had seen the live coverage of the shuttle explosion on Cable News Network (CNN) on January 28, 1986. "According to a *New York Times*/CBS News national survey, 25 percent of 5- to 8-year-olds, 48 percent of 9- to 13-year-olds and 31 percent of 14- to 17-year olds saw the *Challenger* launch at their school that day" (Wright, Kunkel, Pinon & Huston, 1989, p. 27). Monaco and Gaier (1987) chose a natural environment, the classroom, to have the children's regular teacher ask questions and report back to the researchers the children's answers. Five- to 6-year-olds, the youngest group, had a limited understanding of death's permanent nature, but were "sad." For example, "The 5- and 6-year-olds in this study generally portrayed this view: the government or the President will fix things; the problems will be quickly fixed by those in power" (p. 92).

Those 9 and 10 years old were concerned about the cause of death and for the astronaut families. For example, they asked, "How could such a nice person (McAuliffe) die?" and "It's not fair" (Monaco & Gaier, 1987, p. 92). The concerns of the 14- and 15-year-olds were more abstract regarding the consequences of death and the meaning of life. For example, the high school students in the sample

FIG. 4.3. Older children, 9 to 12 years old, fear personal injury and physical destruction as Jackie Todd, age 10, illustrates. Reprinted with permission.

asked, "Are they going to do anything in their memory?" and "If we don't move forward, we've wasted a lot of time and money" (p. 93).

Patterns of Cognition.   Other studies done on children and the *Challenger* disaster looked at gender and cognition as variables with formal features as tools for understanding the message. Wright et al. (1989) asked 9- to 12-year-olds in the fourth, fifth, and sixth grades about their information seeking after the disaster during individual interviews 16 days after the explosion. They found two patterns of response. The first pattern was mostly males and labeled cognitive, although girls did follow this pattern as well. "The most systematically structured variability for boys is concerned with use of space-oriented media and hard knowledge about the shuttle program, leading to impersonal reactions to the event and a cognitive orientation toward further information seeking" (p. 39). The authors said the interview pattern for this fifth-grade boy was typical:

Interviewer: Tell me how you felt when you first saw the explosion of
             Challenger.
Boy: Surprised—I couldn't believe what happened.
Interviewer: What about it made you feel that way?
Boy: The teacher (McAuliffe) worked a long time to get ready for
             this flight ... now there might not be any more space shuttles.
Interviewer: (later in the interview) Why have you kept watching TV news
             about the Challenger?
Boy: Find out what made it explode.
Interviewer: (later) How did you know it was real?
Boy: The President was on every channel talking about it. The
             countdown numbers were on the screen. (p. 39)

The second pattern also was seen with boys and girls, but more so with girls, and was characterized by a high personal involvement with the crew and their family members. This fifth-grade girl's interview is an example of the second pattern.

Interviewer: How did you feel when you first saw the explosion of the
             Challenger?
Girl: Awful ... sad.
Interviewer: What about it made you feel that way?
Girl: All their families and friends watched them die. Everyone
             knew the teacher and her kids were watching. It was horrible.
Interviewer: (later) Why have you kept on watching news about the
             explosion on TV?

Girl: The explosion reminds me of how I feel about it. The teacher was
                on there—could have been Mr. Christie (the science teacher).
Interviewer: (later) How could you tell it was real?
Girl: Teachers were watching TV ... someone screamed ... people
                said, "I can't believe this is really happening." (Wright et al.,
                1989, p. 40)

The children in both patterns knew the *Challenger* explosion was real, but they used different formal features to determine that the reports were real. The children knew how news differs from dramatic presentations on television. Although children may use different formal features to determine what is real, their schemata for factual and fictional television are not separate. Rather, the children's understanding is grounded in what is useful to them in making sense of the world whether the messages are fact or fiction.

Formal Features, Social Inference, and Further Viewing. Some children used formal features and some used social inference features to decide what was real. As in the first pattern, some children used the indications that the television program was real, such as the president on every channel. Video formal features that children said they used to determine the explosion was real included the distance of the camera from the event, the inability to see faces, and the shakiness of the video. Audio formal features included the dead air when the announcer stopped talking and the absence of music. The other important reality cue was social inference, that is, the responses of others such as the behavior of their teachers and responses from other children (Wright et al., 1989).

Approaches to watching further coverage also went along the lines of social and affective or cognitive reasons for continuing to view or not continuing. On the social and affective side, children stopped viewing because they did not want to see people die over and over, and they wanted more on the impact on people and less on the technical aspects. Social and affective reasons for continued viewing included wanting to find out how many people felt and what happened to families of the crew. On the cognitive side, children continued to view because they wanted to know what would happen next, found it interesting, and thought they might see something they had not seen before. Cognitive reasons for not viewing included that there was nothing new (Wright et al., 1989).

The gender-oriented patterns seemed to indicate a sex-role stereotyped response. Perhaps children revert to these patterns of response in situations they have not experienced before (Wright et al., 1989). The differences in responses, however, do not minimize the impact of the experience for all the children: "Whether children focus on the people who die in a disaster and become upset, or adopt a more cognitive orientation whose focus allows them to minimize their expressed feelings, none is immune from the powerful impact of instantly and simultaneously distributed catastrophic news like the Challenger explosion" (Wright et al., 1989, pp. 43–44).

The Gulf War

Although a technological disaster such as the *Challenger* explosion can make an impact on children, wars also leave long memories. The Gulf War, although short, is one that has left its mark. About 1 month after the cease-fire in 1991, Hoffner and Haefner (1994) interviewed third through sixth graders about their reaction and interest in the Gulf War. Just as Wright et al. (1989) found gender-related patterns in the *Challenger* reactions, Hoffner and Haefner (1994) found similar patterns: "Boys reported greater interest in news stories that dealt with the background and technological aspects of the war, whereas girls were more interested in news reports of casualties" (p. 202). Girls also avoided news more, but that was tracked to concern about self and not specifically gender. Both boys and girls

> who felt more personally vulnerable and experienced more enduring upset during the Gulf war reported more interest in neutral/background news (but no casualty news) and avoided exposure to news coverage of the war more often ... Children selectively viewed news stories that helped them to understand the war and to develop a less threatening interpretation of the events (particularly regarding their own safety). (p. 201)

Another Gulf War research project focused on parents' reports of the responses of their children in first, fourth, seventh, and eleventh grades in Madison, Wisconsin (Cantor, Mares, & Oliver, 1993). The children's responses varied by developmental level:

> First graders' questions dealt most frequently with issues of personal safety. Fourth graders reportedly wanted to talk about the war in general, without focusing primarily on issues of personal vulnerability. Questions about global political consequences first appeared in 7th grade, along with questions reflecting a more sophisticated understanding of personal risk, such as questions regarding the draft and the possibility of escalation of the conflict. The comments of children in the 11th grade were the first to show signs of "taking sides" in the conflict, of identifying themselves with the U.S. forces, and of showing less concern for the welfare of non-Americans. (p. 338)

What makes this research striking is that public television viewers had a stronger emotional response than those who did not have that viewing pattern. The authors provided two possible explanations. Perhaps the lessons of programs such as *Sesame Street* or *Mr. Rogers* that teach empathy and concern for others affected the children viewing public television. Another possible explanation is that a third variable such as vocabulary or income level may correlate with public television viewing and emotional response to war coverage (Cantor et al., 1993).

JOURNALISTS AND CHILDREN IN THE NEWS

When children are part of the news, journalists sometimes need help finding appropriate resources on children. The Casey Journalism Center is one of those resources.

Journalists Get Help Covering News Involving Children

When the 6-year-old Michigan boy shot his classmate on Leap Day 2000, journalists all over the country moved to cover the story. To help those journalists, the Casey Journalism Center for Children and Families also had to be ready with sources and research. The Casey Journalism Center aims "to enhance reporting about the issues and institutions affecting disadvantaged children and their families and to increase public awareness about the concerns facing at-risk children."

One of the calls was from National Public Radio reporter Vicky Que, who asked Casey Research Director Jenny Moore which states have child access protection (CAPS) laws for guns. Moore had been one step ahead, anticipating the question and researching the answer just before Que's call. Moore gave Que a list of the 17 states with CAPS laws and an Internet link to read the text of the laws.

In addition to fielding calls, Moore "broadcasts" to a listserv over the Internet with materials the listserv subscribers may find helpful. In addition to the 300 listserv subscribers, the Center has a journalist database that is biographical with contact information for journalists covering children and family issues at some level. They are health writers, crime writers, and education writers. Que covers children and adolescent health and development issues. There are few that have beats that are called children's and family beats (see related sidebar, chapter 3).

Moore compared the Michigan shooting to the school shooting at Columbine. "(The Michigan shooting) seemed to have a different spin," Moore said. "We had done a couple of source lists that we broadcast after the Columbine shootings. When I looked at those, they just didn't seem to fit. They were all about simmering anger, mental health issues, the impact of violent media on children." It differed from Columbine due to "the age of the child and them not knowing whether it was an accidental or an intentional shooting," Moore said. "It being an accidental shooting turned the focus of the story to, 'How did the child get the gun? Why didn't the parents know the child had the gun?' I gave them some school safety resources."

On the day after the Michigan shooting, the story and sources shifted to other angles. "It looks now there is a child welfare connection," Moore said. "So today I may have to follow up with some child welfare sources." For the future, Moore said they are working to get their databases directly available to the journalists they serve.

Casey Journalism Center for Children and Families

Beth Frerking, a working journalist for the *Denver Post* and later Newhouse, became the Director of the Casey Journalism Center for Children and Families because she knew their reputation. "The center had such credibility with journalists," Frerking said. "It is not an advocacy group. It is a neutral entity, and this whole mission of improving coverage of these issues out in the field is important. The Casey Center, I believe is an especially important resource for papers that are not resource rich, but especially for reporters at smaller and midsize papers that do not have the access to Web services, the ability to go to conferences. They may be in the Midwest or in Texas where I grew up, and the better we can educate them, the better the coverage will be. And that serves everyone and it serves children. I think the mission of the center is something I really truck with."

Frerking began her job as director the week the 6-year-old Michigan boy shot his classmate on Leap Day 2000, but she has been working with the Center since she attended the very first national conference sponsored by the Casey Journalism Center. "I was in the first class fellows in '93 pregnant with my second child," Frerking said. "That gave me such a good, concentrated source base, including a lot of more academic researchers that I was not familiar with before that. It sort of gave me a really good harder base for some of the things that I was writing about child development, brain research. It plugged me into the child development, early childhood, child care sort of community, academic research and practice—Families and Work Institute, Ed Ziegler, people like that I had not been familiar with in the past.... I started realizing that if I were to keep specializing in this field, I needed to be aware of what people were doing with research."

The annual conference pays for journalists as fellows to attend the conference on topics such as child care, children's health, child abuse, welfare reform, and violence. Both academic researchers and policymakers also attend the conference to provide their expertise.

"We hope to create an environment where the researchers learn from the journalists and the journalists learn from the researchers," Casey Research Director Jenny Moore said of the annual conference the Casey Center sponsors. "One of the most important questions we ask the researchers—and all the journalists get their pens ready—'What story ideas do you have? What do you want to see covered that's not being covered?'"

The Casey Journalism Center is there to help. Frerking wants to go beyond the children and family reporters to any reporter who may work on a story about children. "I want to take it to that next level," Frerking said. "That means increasing visibility in the industry. Someone who covers demographics could use us. They probably don't know about us because they are not children and family reporters. So I want to get to those people."

STRATEGIES FOR REDUCING FEARS

Adults need to know how children react to messages inducing fear at different ages, but they also need strategies for reducing fears as the child develops (see Fig. 4.4). For preschool children, noncognitive strategies that involve showing or doing instead of explaining are best. Older children prefer cognitive or talk-related methods, although noncognitive methods are also effective with older children. The noncognitive strategy that is perhaps best known is simply not looking by covering one's eyes. In addition, various forms of distraction are familiar. Holding an object such as a "blankey" or eating something (chewing can help to reduce stress) can be effective ways to reduce fear in small and sometimes not-so-small children. Although verbal explanations (cognitive) do not work because children are too young to understand concepts, a visual desensitization, such as letting children view the Incredible Hulk character putting on his makeup, can be effective (Cantor, 1996).

For older children, cognitive strategies can be effective: "Cognitive strategies involve verbal explanations or instructions that encourage the child to think about

FIG. 4.4.   Children look to adults to reduce fears, as they compare fantasy to reality in their lives. JEFF STAHLER reprinted by permission of Newspaper Enterprise Association, Inc.

the fear stimulus in a way that casts the threat in a different light" (Cantor, 1996, p. 104). For an older child, explaining why something is not real, such as the flying monkeys in *The Wizard of Oz*, is effective in reducing fear. Or, as in the case of *The Incredible Hulk*, telling children how makeup helps to make things scary is effective for older children. However, sometimes the threats are real. In this case, the cognitive strategy is to explain that the danger is not likely or as severe as depicted. Researchers have found it effective to provide information about snakes, for example, such as that most snakes are not poisonous, for those children viewing *Raiders of the Lost Ark*. Older children also choose cognitive strategies on their own, such as talking to an adult about a program, as researchers found in their study of *The Day After*, a drama about a nuclear war (Cantor, 1996).

Cognitive strategies do not work with younger children specifically because they do not yet have the cognitive skills. Younger children may not understand the words used to quantify, such as the word *some* or conditional terms such as *possibly*. In addition, for small children, things are what they appear to be, such that attractive characters are good and unattractive characters are bad. "It is extremely difficult to communicate to young children that something that looks scary is, in fact, benign and something that looks attractive is really dangerous" (Cantor, 1996, pp. 110–111).

It is clear that some of this information is not intuitive. We may think that a young child, for example, would be afraid of a program about a nuclear holocaust. However, if the fear is not visually scary to the small child, like a monster would be, then the child may be less frightened than an older child or an adult.

SEPTEMBER 11, 2001

The millennial generation of children include the coming-of-age young adults for the most recent news trauma, the events of September 11, 2001. Generation Z will live in a post-September 11 world. In her speech to the National Press Club, First Lady Laura Bush gave this perspective on the trauma for children's lives:

> If we set aside one day for each victim, to honor and remember them, it would take us 13 or 14 years to complete the tribute. Or to put it another way, a child born on September 11th would be entering high school by the time we were through with our days of remembrance. (Bush, 2001)

The mass media were the way many saw the collapsing of the World Trade Center towers, including children. In addition to providing the visuals of the trauma, the mass media, including the Internet, also provided advice for parents about what to look for in children during the period after the trauma.

The *Harvard Mental Health Letter* gave grief or trauma symptoms and advice on how to talk to children by age level. Up to age 6, children may be clingy and require more attention from adults. Children may regress to behaviors they have outgrown, such as bed wetting and thumb sucking. Other symptoms include stomachaches, headaches, or not being hungry. Very young children should not be exposed to repeated televised viewing. They may even think the event is happening over again or that they are in danger. Props like toy ambulances or fire trucks that may help children explain their feelings can be useful. From ages 6 to 11, children may feel guilty and responsible for the source of the trauma or grief. They may repeat play related to the trauma. They may do poorly in school and display behaviors such as irritability and lack of concentration. Older children can understand cognitively about death but will need many assurances that they will be okay and that the fearful feelings are normal and will go away over time. Teens may be rebellious and act as though they do not care. They may take risks, act antisocially, or withdraw. Acting like they don't care may be a way to empower themselves when they feel powerless. Teens can talk to adults and friends to get through the trauma ("Disaster and Trauma," 2002).

Art is another way children can cope with a trauma. The Internet has begun to archive children's art at sites such as Artsonia, which claims to be the largest student art museum on the Internet. They show art from 90 countries by more than 20,000 students. After September 11, Artsonia created a collection called "Drawing Together: Kids Against Terrorism." The art is from around the world and can be accessed at www.artsonia.com/dtkat. Some believe art activity can help by empowering the children to express their ideas and feelings in their own ways: "Out of this pain and tragedy of what happened, these students came to experience their own strength and opportunity for personal growth—they could transcend tragedy through their own action" (Felton & Hausman, 2002). Mass media images can rob children of their own creativity and their own perceptions as passive recipients. "What is important is that we not look away from what is happening. What is just as important is that we think and act and feel in ways that honor our own integrity and humanity" (Felton & Hausman, 2002). (See the list of Web sites on topic at the end of the chapter.)

FICTIONALIZED NEWS

Because news is real, children may be more vulnerable to it. However it gets confusing for the child viewer when a story that could be real is presented as fiction. The child viewer may need more skills than some children have and scare the adults more than the children. Research on *The Day After*, a story about a nuclear war, shows that when younger children are not interested in or do not understand an abstract concept, they will not be fearful. The research on *The Day After* differs from research on other events in that fright increased with age instead of decreasing. Yet, parental restrictions decreased as children got older. Because the movie was not as interesting to the younger children, many did not view it to the end. The concept of nuclear holocaust was too abstract for younger children as well. All these factors contributed to children's lack of fear and emotional upset (Cantor, 1992).

ADVERTISING AND THE PROGRAM-LENGTH COMMERCIAL

Whereas children may react with fear to crisis news and violent visuals, they react to advertising that targets them, particularly ads for toys, with the urge to own. The younger child does not understand the difference between fantasy entertainment and the real appeal. The toys also may seem real to the younger child just as the Velveteen Rabbit did to the child in the nursery in the story we began this chapter with. Children use toys as tools for their imagination and play, their essential work as children. However, if the toys are linked to a mass media event such as a television program, do children imitate the program or do children use the toys to exercise their own imaginations?

If children have a hard time with news and reality-based fiction, they also have a difficult time with program-length commercials or host selling because the perceptual cues or formal features are the same for the fantasy program and the ad. If a Pokemon character, for example, is both performing in the program and in the ads selling toys and other products, where does the program end and the ad begin? The research literature establishes the fact that "children below the age of about 5 have difficulty differentiating commercials from programs" (Wilson & Weiss, 1992, p. 373). When children can differentiate between show and ad, it is because there are perceptual cues that tip them off. Developmentally, children do not realize selling intent until age 7 or 8. The more ads children see, especially younger children, the more products they want and the more they try to influence their parents to purchase those products (Wilson & Weiss, 1992). In experiments trying to separate programs from ads, younger children, ages 4 to 6, did do a better job differentiating program from ad when the program was not a toy-based cartoon. However, simply separating the ad from the program did not help the younger children. The researchers concluded, "It is the shared formal features in the ads and cartoons that are causing the confusion, and not the relative placement of the two related messages" (Wilson & Weiss, 1992, p. 391).

Other research on program-length commercials has found that children's skills shift at age 7 or 8 regarding the use of the television material in their fantasy life as well: "The majority of research on television and imagination indicates a detrimental effect of the medium" (Greenfield et al., 1993, p. 55). In their experiment to determine the effects of host selling on children in first and second grades, Greenfield et al. (1993) used Smurf toys and Smurf cartoons. They defined imagination as "any form of representational activity that creates entities or events not found in the present or immediately preceding stimulus situation" (p. 58). For these researchers, transcendent imagination includes both creative imagination and imitative imagination. What they found is that product-based television encouraged more imitation than creativity for some children. Like other researchers in this field, Greenfield et al. (1993) concluded that "television elicits more recall-oriented and fewer creative responses than other media" (p. 69). However, the authors did not expect the dramatic difference between the first and second graders in the study:

> The combination of thematically related toys plus cartoons leads to the highest production of character dialogue for first graders, whereas the same combination leads to the lowest production of character dialogue for second graders.... The results support the idea that television, particularly when combined with thematically related toys, functions as a cultural tool that aids the imaginative development of younger children. (Greenfield et al., 1993, p. 67)

It is interesting to note that the authors concluded that these younger children use television to help them develop their imagination skills:

> We found that television (especially combined with thematically related toys) stimulated the transcendent imagination of mental events for the younger child not yet able to do it on his or her own, whereas it dampened the transcendent imagination of mental events for the older child with more advanced cognitive skills. Therefore, we would predict that television would stimulate the creative imagination of physical events for an even younger child not yet able to imaginatively create physical events on is or her own.... Our results suggest that the television, as well as TV-based toys, are potent cultural tools for developing the symbolic representation of mental events. (Greenfield et al., 1993, p. 70)

Thus the effects of even host selling can shift as the child's developmental needs shift. At early stages, product-based advertising can help develop imagination, but when cognitive skills are developed, the benefit quickly becomes a detriment to the development of the child's imagining skills.

SUMMARY

Children's ability to differentiate reality from fantasy is at the crux of the development of children's relationship to mass media. Whether it is their responses to news events or advertising, the ability for children to use the messages for their own development follows patterns based on age, level of cognition, and gender. Responses may include fear, further searching for information, product purchases, imitation, or creativity.

FOR FURTHER CONSIDERATION

1. Davies (1997) cited Jerome Bruner and his attempt to identify schemas by having the subjects tell back a classic story, such as Little Red Riding Hood. Write your own version of a classic story. Analyze your story for "schemas

of interpretation." (Davies, 1997, p. 40). For application by Bruner see Susan Neumann, *Literacy in the Television Age* (Davies, 1997, pp. 41–42).

2. Write a report on one program, film, or event in the mass media that scared you (Cantor, 1996, p. 108).

3. View the video *Merchants of Cool* and explain how teens can both be rebellious toward adult authority and also emulate the images in the media presented by adults.

RESOURCES ON THE WEB

- American Academy of Child & Adolescent Psychiatry (www.aacap.org)
- Artsonia exhibit "Drawing Together: Kids Against Terrorism" (www.artsonia.com/dtkat)
- Resource and study guide to spark discussions on media's role in covering September 11 (http://web.mit.edu/cms/reconstructions)
- International Reading Association's Helping children respond Web page (http://www.reading.org/links/crisis_resources.html)
- PBS (www.pbs.org/americaresponds/parents.html)
- American Academy of Pediatrics (www.aap.org)

REFERENCES

Bush, L. (2001, December 1). What do you say to children? *Vital Speeches of the Day 68* [Electronic version]. Retrieved July 1, 2001, from EBSCOhost.

Cantor, J. (1992). Children's emotional reactions to technological disasters conveyed by mass media. In J. M. Wober (Ed.), *Television and nuclear power: Making the public mind* (pp. 31–53). Norwood, NJ: Ablex.

Cantor, J. (1996). Television and children's fear. In T. McBeth (Ed.), *Tuning in to young viewers: Social science perspectives on television* (pp. 87–115). Thousand Oaks, CA: Sage.

Cantor, J., Mares, M., & Oliver, M. B. (1993). Parents' and children's emotional reactions to TV coverage of the Gulf War. In B. S. Greenberg & W. Gantz (Eds.), *Desert Storm and the mass media* (pp. 325–340). Cresskill, NJ: Hampton.

Davies, M. M. (1997). *Fake, fact, and fantasy, children's interpretation of television reality.* Mahwah, NJ: Lawrence Erlbaum Associates.

Disaster and trauma. (2002, January). *Harvard Mental Health Letter, 18* [Electronic version]. Retrieved February 8, 2002, from EBSCOhost.

Felton, R., & Hausman, J. J. (2002, January). Transcending tragedy. *Arts and Activities, 130.* Retrieved February 8, 2002, from EBSCOhost.

Greenfield, P. M., Yut, E., Chung, M., Land, D., Kreider, H., & Pantoja, M., et al. (1993). The program-length commercial: A study of the effects of television/toy tie-ins on imaginative play. In G. L. Berry & J. K. Asamen (Eds.), *Children and television: Images in a changing sociocultural world* (pp. 53–72). Newbury Park, CA: Sage.

Hoffner, C., & Haefner, M. J. (1994, Spring). Children's news interest during the Gulf War: The role of negative affect. *Journal of Broadcasting and Electronic Media, 38,* 193–204.

Monaco, N. M., & Gaier, E. L. (1987). Developmental level and children's responses to the explosion of the space shuttle Challenger. *Early Childhood Research Quarterly, 2,* 83–95.

Williams, M. (1958). *The velveteen rabbit, or how toys become real*. New York: Doubleday.

Wilson, B. J., & Weiss, A. J. (1992, Fall). Developmental differences in children's reactions to a toy advertisement linked to a toy-based cartoon. *Journal of Broadcasting and Electronic Media, 36*, 371–394.

Wright, J. C., Kunkel, D., Pinon, M., & Huston, A. C. (1989, Spring). How children reacted to televised coverage of the space shuttle disaster. *Journal of Communication, 39*, 27–45.

CHAPTER FIVE

Effects

Chance went inside and turned on the TV. The set created its own light, its own color, own time. It did not follow the law of gravity that forever bent all plants downward. Everything on TV was tangled and mixed and yet smoothed out: night and day, big and small, tough and brittle, soft and rough, hot and cold, far and near....

By changing the channel he could change himself. He could go through phases, as garden plants went through phases, but could change as rapidly as he wished by twisting the dial backward and forward.... By turning the dial, Chance could bring others inside his eyelids. Thus he came to believe it was he, Chance, and no one else, who made himself be.

... Though Chance could not read or write, he resembled the man on TV more than he differed from him....

He sank into the screen. Like sunlight and fresh air and mild rain, the world from outside the garden entered Chance, and Chance, like a TV image, floated into the world, buoyed up by a force he did not see and could not name. (Kosinski, 1970, pp. 5–6)

In *Being There,* Chance the gardener is an adult but has many characteristics of a child. For this man, TV seems to be his only socializing agent because he seems to have no family and no friends. Here fantasy and reality are the same for this man who seems to be caught in the early childhood developmental stage. Kosinski (1970) seems to develop this book based on the question, what if TV raised children? What would they look like? What would be the effects?

Effects are difficult to measure because human beings are complex and children cannot necessarily tell us what they are thinking or why they act as they do. One author compared children's introduction to television to a man blind from birth who can see after an operation:

To a normal child, the introduction to the world through the images of television represents a similar confusing experience. Television is a new language of sight and sound that carries, in rapid-fire succession, a wide variety of messages and impressions about the real and imaginary worlds that television portrays. At first, there are no clear lines separating one world from the other. The child calls out to the nearest interpreter for clarification: "Daddy, did that man really die?" "No, that was only a story. It's only make believe." And once again, when what seems like a similar message repeats itself: "Mommy, did that man really die?" "I'm afraid so, dear, you're watching the news." And so for a child, the gradual decoding of life as seen on TV begins with one of the first lessons: news carries messages that are real and unsettling. As they get older, children begin to understand that this real world they see on TV is full of problems, people, and events over which they have little influence but which must be understood so they can survive in today's society. They also learn at an early age they can control these difficult television challenges by turning the dial to another station. (Heller, 1982, pp. 31–32)

Turning the channel with a remote control was the mode that Chance the gardener tried to alter real life when he escaped his home in the movie *Being There* (Ashby, 1979). However, he could not change life with a remote. For children, also, there are often no choices that allow escape from TV messages that can be harmful. The concerns for children's welfare vis-á-vis mass media have a history that begins with radio, reflecting the audience's perceptions of possible harm and researchers' findings of possible harm as well as the response of the media industry and the government.

A HISTORY OF CONCERNS WITH MEDIA EFFECTS: AUDIENCE, RESEARCHERS, INDUSTRY, AND GOVERNMENT

1930s–1940s

Concerns about the relationship between media and children began when radio entered homes and became the first electronic mass medium to be a home utility and adults in the audience called for restraint. In 1933, a Scarsdale, New York, parent organization "called for an end to the 'Ether Bogeyman' that was causing nightmares and other emotional problems among their young children" (Cooper, 1996, p. 21). The Scarsdale group did a survey of parents and found parents could find only 5 of 40 children's radio shows acceptable for their children. The parents said that even *Betty Boop* and *Little Orphan Annie* were unacceptable due to stories, some violent, that "'keep children in emotional suspense and excite them so they can't sleep'" (Cooper, 1996, p. 22).

1950s

The nightmares continued with the beginning of television. The specific concern in the 1950s was with the problem of juvenile delinquency. In addition to parents blaming television for the juvenile behavior, juvenile offenders also blamed television (Cooper, 1996, p. 28). Battle lines between those who blamed television for youth violence and aggression and those who believed the media were scapegoats for these problems were drawn:

> Adolescent psychologist Erik Erikson called television a "scapegoat" for those searching for an immediate and simplistic fix to a problem that really had not been thoroughly researched. Columnist Goodman Ace wrote that the campaign against television was just the latest in a long tradition of blaming a mass medium for the ills of society. (Cooper, 1996, p. 30)

In 1955 the federal government responded with hearings by the U.S. Senate Subcommittee to Investigate Juvenile Delinquency, including an investigation of television. In the testimony, researchers noted a number of the roots of later findings. Elenor Maccoby, a researcher at Harvard, found both that mothers liked the freedom they got when they could let their children watch television (i.e., babysit) and that mothers did notice their younger children were more aggressive after watching TV. Dr. Ralph Banay, a psychiatric consultant to the Bureau of Prisons, noted that he believed, "Television violence was particularly harmful to emotionally disturbed children because they were the most prone to delinquent behavior. Banay analogized that as prison was often described as a college for crime, television was a preparatory school for delinquency" (Cooper, 1996, p. 31). Like many hearing groups that followed, the subcommittee led by Senator Estes Kefauver concluded concern over television was justified, but more research was needed.

The industry also addressed concerns about the content of media messages by adopting a television code that acknowledged its responsibility toward children, which was accepted by the National Association of Broadcasters (NAB) in 1956:

> "Responsibility Toward Children: The education of children involves giving them a sense of the world at large. Crime, violence and sex are a part of the world they will be called upon to meet, and a certain amount of proper presentation of such is helpful in orienting the child to his social surroundings. However, violence and illicit sex shall not be presented in an attractive manner, nor to an extent such as will lead children to believe that they play a greater part in life than they do. They should not be represented without indications of the resultant retribution and punishment." (Cooper, 1996, p. 34)

The code certainly identified the correct parameters for their own presentations, as later research would point out:

1. Do not show attractive depictions of violence or illicit sex.
2. Do show results of violent and sexual behavior.

TV would have been a lot different if these guidelines had been followed. (In 1983, the NAB eliminated their code.)

1960s

By 1961, however, government critics found television still lacking in responsibility to the viewers. FCC Commissioner Newton Minow castigated the landscape of television in a speech to the NAB:

> "When television is bad, nothing is worse. I invite you to sit in front of your television when your station goes on the air and stay there ... until the station signs off. I can assure you that you will observe a vast wasteland. You will see a procession of game shows, violence, audience participation shows, formula comedies about totally unbelievable families, blood and thunder, mayhem, violence, sadism, murder, Western badmen, Western good men, private eyes, gangsters, more violence and cartoons." (Cooper, 1996, pp. 37–38)

Minow concluded, "'To those few broadcasters who would evade the nation's needs and cry "Censorship! Oh where will it end?" there can only be one answer: "Responsibility—when will it begin?"'" (pp. 38–39).

Besides industry responsibility, research played a role in the debate over effects. Research seems to direct advertisers in spending millions of dollars on advertising for the attention of children to the mass media. A question asked in 1961 Congressional hearings linked advertising focus with effects on behavior: "If, as broadcasters claimed, television had so much influence over the buying habits of children, why did it not have the same level of influence regarding behavior?" (Cooper, 1996, p. 40). Schramm testified at these hearings in 1961 regarding researcher views of effects and included his ideas in *Television in the Lives of Our Children*. His summary applies today as well:

> For *some* children, under *some* conditions, *some* television is harmful. For *other* children under the same conditions, or for the same children under *other* conditions, it may be beneficial. For *most* children, under *most* conditions, *most* television is probably neither particularly harmful nor particularly beneficial. (Schramm, Lyle, & Parker, 1961, p. 1)

Much of the research that continues today is an effort to define who and what the *some*, *other*, and *most* are in each of these cases.

1970s

By 1972, the concerns for television effects had been addressed in *Television and Growing Up: The Impact of Television Violence; Report of the Surgeon General* (U.S. Surgeon General's Scientific Advisory Committee on Television and Social

Behavior, 1972). This report, like many that followed, examined the research to date, summarized it, and made an evaluation of the status of our understanding of the effects of the media. Because violence is a health concern, the U.S. Surgeon General, among others, takes on the job of such a report. The report concluded television was only one possible factor in violent behavior, except for those "pre-disposed to aggressive behavior," who, the broadcasters claimed, would be violent in any case (Cooper, 1996, p. 72). The U.S. Surgeon General's Report (1972) influenced Williams (1986) in the development of a Canadian study of the effects on a community comparing behaviors before and after it received television. The situation allowed for a natural experiment comparing three communities: the one acquiring television (Notel) compared to one with a single channel (Unitel) and another with multiple channels (Multitel) in Canada. The conclusions of the research emphasized the effects of displacement. Displacement is the most easily proven because we know that when children choose to use mass media, they are not choosing other types of activity like playing outside with their friends (see Fig. 5.1). For children, the research documented how television displaced reading and affected use of leisure time and community activities.

FIG. 5.1.   Screen time, whether television or video games, displaces other activities the child could be doing. TOLES © The Buffalo News. Reprinted by permission of UNIVERSAL PRESS SYNDICATE. All rights reserved.

1980s

Ten years after the U.S. Surgeon General's Report (1972), researcher Jerome Singer, in a 1982 National Institute of Mental Health (NIMH) report, suggested that research was accumulating to reconsider television as a critical element in children's environment. Singer (1982) supported the underlying need for children to organize their learning with television as a major factor:

> We must recognize that children are growing up in an environment in which they must learn to organize experiences and emotional responses not only in relationship to the physical and social environment of the home but also in relation to the omnipresent 21-inch screen that talks, sings, dances, and encourages the desire for toys, candies, and breakfast foods. (p. 2)

The research suggested that adults needed to pay more attention to the role of television in children's lives than had been acknowledged in the early 1970s.

1990s

By 1992, the CTA became law (see chapter 9) and an American Psychological Association (APA) task force on television and society had reviewed the research literature and come up with its recommendations. The populations with which the task force was concerned by 1992 were children, the elderly, women, and minorities.

The task force made three basic assumptions:

1. All television is educational television.

2. Television often influences viewers by ... the "drip" model, a process of subtle and gradual incorporation of frequent and repeated messages.

3. Effects of television on any individual depend on the characteristics and goals of the viewer as well as the content of what is watched.... One implication of this assumption is that changing the effects of television depends on interventions with viewers as well as changes in what is available to view. (Huston et al., 1992, p. 6)

Thus the assumptions as well as the ideas researchers used had become more complex and had moved from focusing on the message to focusing on the viewer or receiver of the message.

2000 and Beyond

Almost 30 years after the 1972 Surgeon General's report on television and human behavior, there was a second Surgeon General's report on youth violence. It is important to note that this report was not focused on media but on youth violence, a switch in context and emphasis. The events at Columbine High School in April 1999, resulting in 15 deaths including the two perpetrators and one teacher, motivated the 2001 report called for by both the president and Congress.

The conclusion of the Surgeon General's 2001 report was that media violence may lead to some aggression but there is little evidence it leads to violence (U.S. Department of Health and Human Services, 2001, p. 65). The report emphasized that it is aggression, not violence that may be motivated by mass media. Aggression is "an outcome that psychologists define as any behavior, physical or verbal, that is intended to harm another person.... The label 'violence' is reserved for the most extreme end of the physical aggression spectrum" (p. 87). The mass media are part of many factors affecting the aggression outcome: "The influence of the mass media, however strong or weak, is best viewed as one of the many potential factors that help to shape behavior, including violent behavior" (p. 87).

Next we turn to the various tools and theories researchers used to establish the effects of the media.

TOOLS OF THE SOCIAL SCIENTIST

The tools social science researchers have used to determine effects are related to the elements of the communication model discussed earlier. Strasburger (1995) listed six types of communication research: attitudinal surveys, content analyses, naturalistic experiments, lab experiments, field experiments, and correlational studies.

The attitudinal surveys look specifically at the receiver or audience. Surveys are self-reports and as such have the drawback of the error of receivers giving their self-perceptions. In addition, the survey is difficult to administer to younger children and requires the permission of parents. It is a challenge to gather accurate data from the perspective of the child receiver.

Content analyses look specifically at the message of the communication. The content analysis can say nothing specific about the effects the message might have on the receiver. It is a danger for the researcher to deduce that because a message is bad, the effects are bad. Because content analyses are relatively easy to conduct, there are a lot of them and their numbers continue to put a lot of emphasis on the message and the oldest of the models for determining effects: the bullet theory. The bullet theory is also called the direct effects model or the hypodermic needle theory. This theory says that the message's effects are felt directly without change from the nature of the message or even the intent of the source. It is as if a bullet is shot and hits the receiver without any interference or a receiver were shot with a hypodermic needle with the message the source wanted delivered.

Naturalistic experiments are the ones we can conduct because of a natural opportunity, as did Williams (1986) when she set up the Notel examination of the community in Canada both before and after it had received television (see earlier). Lab experiments try to deal with causality by isolating variables, using comparison groups, and controlling the experiment. However, the control itself tends to create an artificial situation. For example, Bandura's BoBo doll experiment (see chapter 1) was conducted in a lab situation. The children were not at home; they were put into a room with a BoBo doll following a film showing an individual beating up a BoBo doll and in one case being rewarded. The fact that most children in that situation beat up the BoBo doll may provide evidence for imitation, but it does not prove that a child will beat up another child as a result of seeing a BoBo doll beat up, especially because the BoBo doll is made for the purpose of being punched and is not a sentient being. Lab experiments are artificial and difficult to generalize to another situation.

Field experiments try to gain the best of the experiment while trying for a more natural setting. Some field experiments even have been conducted in teen girls' bedrooms to get them at ease with making responses and explaining their use of media. Field experiments may be longitudinal studies of children as they grow up, comparing descriptions and surveys from time to time.

Correlation Is Not Causation: The Chicken and the Egg

Correlational studies correlate data such as population attributes (e.g., heavy or light viewers) with self-reports of groups (e.g., aggressive behavior of the individual) to determine if there is a relationship between the population attribute and the behavior or attitude. For example, do heavy viewers of violent or aggressive images act violently or aggressively themselves? However, we are never sure which came first—the chicken or the egg. Do aggressive children choose to view violent media or do violent media cause children to be aggressive? Correlation is not causation and the relationship between the media and the individual receiver can be very complex.

MacBeth (1996) described the chicken and egg problem this way:

> How can we figure out whether people who differ on some dimension, for example, aggressive behavior or creativity or reading skills, use TV differently, or whether watching TV or watching certain kinds of programs affects viewers' behavior in those areas? (p. 16)

One possible explanation is that the child is aggressive and chooses to consume aggressive media. A second explanation is that the aggressive media cause the child to be aggressive. A third option is that both behaviors are caused by a separate variable such as parents' supervision or lack thereof. A fourth option is "that the relationship goes both ways and is transactional" (p. 17).

The bidirectional explanation is one way to avoid the chicken and egg problem. In his research on TV violence and aggression, Huesmann (1986) effectively described what he called a reciprocal developmental process. Huesmann said the chicken and the egg problem does not exist here. Rather, an interaction exists between the television viewing and the aggression: Aggression increases with viewing and viewing increases with aggression.

Researchers trying to predict cause and effect use a variety of these tools to provide evidence that supports theories we have examined. For example, researchers using cultivation theory (see chapter 1) combine content analyses of the messages and attitudinal surveys of the audience. Researchers supporting social learning theory also use content analysis and attitudinal surveys.

A specific example of researchers wrestling with the problem of causality is a recent report on the relationship of teen sexuality and soap operas and MTV programming. "Whether sexual permissiveness is influenced by exposure to SSM (soaps and MTV), or permissive persons select provocative media is not known" (Strouse & Buerkel-Rothfuss, 1993, p. 290). With evidence from cultivation research, findings in antisocial effects of violent media, and script theory (see later), the researchers carefully concluded the media are the cause of violence: "We cautiously suggest that in our culture of sexual double standards, religiosity restrains and SSM accelerates sexual permissiveness more for females than for males, and sexual 'scoring' enhances the self-esteem of males more than females" (Strouse & Buerkel-Rothfuss, 1993, p. 292).

THEORIES USED IN EFFECTS RESEARCH

Message-Based Theories

Much of the literature refers to cultivation research (as in the sexual permissiveness research just mentioned) or learning theory as its theoretical base. We examined cultivation theory and learning theory in chapter 1. Cultivation theory is based on the longest content analysis of television programming in the history of media research, which began in the 1960s. Content analyses examine the message of the communication process. Some researchers, however, differ with the assumptions of the research. Brown (1993) said cultivation analysis assumes that content is uniform across programming. To get around this problem, the sexuality research just cited looks specifically at soaps and MTV. Thus the more recent research helps to define limits in theories and tries to use the strength of the current research while continuing to use the original theories. In addition to narrowing the type of programming to the types used by teens, the researchers in the soaps and MTV example also looked specifically at teen attitudes about the programming, thus including the receiver in the message-based research (Brown, 1993).

Research on Violence: Content and Exposure

We turn next to a major research project to demonstrate what current findings are, what methods are used, and how the theories have worked to help interpret and predict those findings in violence research. The National Television Violence Study compiles several studies. In the first examined here, the authors used

FIG. 5.2. Bullying is one manifestation of violence in children's lives as Christian Incandella, age 9, illustrates. Reprinted by permission.

profiles and risk composites in an attempt to characterize children's programming content that may result in violent behavior.

Wilson et al. (1998) used a content analysis of programming and developmental psychology theory to determine what the authors call risk composites for two different age groups: children under 7 and older children and teens. By specifically locating types of programming with characteristics that might impact children at various ages, the research provides the relationship between the programming and the child by age. Although content analysis does not establish cause and effect, because it looks only at the message, the researchers can provide a match between the risks of children and different ages and the programming they have examined.

To begin, the researchers provided a developmental progression for children based on earlier research. On the issue of reality, children begin at 2 or 3 years old seeing no differences between television and the real world, even talking to the TV characters as if they were real. By preschool, children judge reality by whether it looks real to them. Although preschoolers may acknowledge verbally that cartoons are not real, their reactions to the characters seem to treat those characters as if they were real. As children grow older, they judge reality by their experiences and whether the depicted characters and events could occur in real life (Wilson et al., 1998).

The researchers justified two risk composites based on these developmental differences. Younger and older children differ on perceptions of reality and ability to integrate information. Due to their developmental skills, younger children may be more susceptible to fantasy-based and animation-based violence, but older children and teens disregard these portrayals as being not real. Younger children do not do as well as older children at linking disjointed segments and character behaviors (Wilson et al., 1998).

High Risk Composites.   Younger children are at high risk for susceptibility to the media that may facilitate aggression using the following variables:

1. Whether the perpetrator is *attractive*.
2. Whether the violence is *justified*.
3. Whether the violence is *rewarded or punished* immediately after it occurs.
4. Whether *harm and pain* is shown.
5. Whether the portrayal is likely to be perceived as *realistic* (Wilson et al., 1998, p. 129).

The older children and adolescents composite differed on Variables 3 and 5: For older children, reward or punishment did not need to be immediate (Variable 3). However, punishment or some response on the part of the aggressor such as remorse did need to be shown to avoid the risk of an aggressive viewer response. For Variable 5, the older children could judge whether the violence was realistic and, if it was, then the older child would be more susceptible to some effect (Wilson et al., 1998). Realism is defined by all three factors of "live action, human characters, and authentic plot" (p. 132).

Programming Compared to Risk Composites.   The researchers then used these composites to examine their content analyses of programming. They found that young children were at the highest risk for negative effects from the type of programming that we call children's programming. Nearly all of the high-risk aggressions found in the content analysis were in animated programs (92%):

> In other words, *cartoons are largely responsible for the concentration of problematic portrayals in children's programming.* These animated stories frequently feature the pattern of violence that is likely to encourage aggression in children under 7 years of age: an attractive perpetrator engaging in justified violence that is rarely punished and produces minimal consequences. (Wilson et al., 1998, p. 135)

For older children the highest risk programming content was drama and movies often seen in prime-time television because these depictions are realistic. Aggressive characters are attractive, are not punished, and do not express any remorse. Consequences of the aggression are minimal. Drama and movie portrayals of aggression may teach and reinforce aggression among older children. The programming with the minimum of risk for older children are comedies, children's programming, music videos, and reality-based shows (Wilson et al., 1998). The conclusions are that children are most susceptible to the type of programming they are most likely to be watching—younger children to cartoons and older children and teens to prime-time drama.

Receiver-Based Theories: Schemata Theory

Although the research on the content of the message even with a clear developmental theory base is an important consideration for effects studies, effects must be grounded in how the audience is impacted by the message in addition to potential risk of exposure. Receiver-based theories such as schemata theory strive to provide us with effects on the audience. Schemata theory is sometimes referred to as script theory and states that the receiver will choose information that reinforces his or her attitudes or beliefs. Schemata theory examines the receiver of the message and assumes models, beliefs, and expectations guide human behavior:

> This information-processing and behavior-directing model (is called) schema ... The model, belief or expectation is actively constructed by the individual, based on experience. Once established, it is used to process new information—upon encountering something ... the individual searches mentally for a schema or script into which to fit the information. (Williams, 1986, pp. 403–404)

Schemata then influence the way information is processed:

> From this perspective, a child or adolescent would be expected not simply to adopt attitudes and behaviors he or she has seen rewarded in TV programs, but actively to seek out "information about gender roles and then monitor his or her own behavior so that it is consistent with the gender-role norms." (Walsh-Childers & Brown, 1993, pp. 118–119)

Thus schemata theory involves the receivers in actively seeking information and monitoring their own behaviors.

> Some teens appear to seek out programs that can provide information and role models salient to their developing understanding of male–female relationships. Adolescents also may use similar information and role models for very different purposes, depending on their initial beliefs about relationships. (Walsh-Childers & Brown, 1993, p. 133)

Schemata theory is often used in research having to do with socialization, including research on violence and on sexuality.

Research on Violence: Schema and Long-Term Effects

The effects of violence can be seen as either short-term or long-term effects. The Surgeon General's Youth Violence Report, discussed earlier, concluded that the laboratory experimental research supports the short-term effects: "Brief exposure to violent dramatic presentations on television or films causes short-term increases in the aggressive behavior of youths, including physically aggressive behavior" (U.S. Department of Health and Human Services, 2001, p. 89). However, what about the long-term effects? These are more difficult to research and more difficult to prove.

Eron and Huesmann (1984) followed a group for 22 years and then applied developmental reciprocal theory to account for their findings. First, they asked 8-year-olds to identify aggressiveness in their peers and checked with the same individuals as adults 22 years later:

> The more aggressive child was one who, according to his or her peers, pushes and shoves other children, starts fights over nothing, always gets into trouble, etc. The study revealed that the children who were rated as more aggressive by their peers at age 8 were more likely to be convicted of crimes by age 30, and if convicted, had on the average committed more serious crimes. They were also more likely to abuse physically their spouses and children, and more likely to have been convicted of moving traffic violations including drunk driving. (Huesmann, 1986, p. 128)

In this longitudinal study looking at 8-year-olds and the same individuals more than 20 year later, Eron and Huesmann (1984) found "TV violence scores at age 8 do themselves predict ... serious antisocial behaviors 22 years later" (p. 146). The researchers were able to predict based on TV violence viewing and frequency of TV viewing at age 8 which male participants would be aggressive, would have committed serious crimes, and the extent of aggressive behavior while drinking at age 30. The prediction did not hold true for female participants. However, for the females at age 30, the researchers found television violence "correlated positively with ratings at age 30 of how severely they punished their children" (Eron & Huesmann, 1984, p. 149). In addition, the researchers followed the children of the original participants and found a relationship between the original participants' television viewing and aggression and their children's television viewing and aggression:

> There is a correlation ... between the subjects' violence viewing at age 8, and their children's violence viewing 22 years later. Even more impressive is the correlation ... between the subjects' violence viewing at age 8 and their children's self-rated aggression 22 years later. Television is indeed a powerful *teacher*. What the subject learns about life from the television screen seems to be transmitted to the next generation. (p. 151)

Huesmann's (1986) developmental theory provides the specifics of the reciprocal relationship between television violence and aggression. TV violence viewing leads to aggression and more violence viewing, which establish schemas or scripts for children whose behavior continues with aggression in their adult lives.

The effect of media violence on individual differences in aggression is primarily the result of a cumulative learning process during childhood. Aggressive scripts for behavior are acquired from observation of media violence and aggressive behavior itself stimulates the observation of media violence. In both childhood and adulthood, certain cues in the media may trigger the activation of aggressive scripts acquired in any manner and thus stimulate aggressive behavior. A number of intervening variables may mitigate or exacerbate these reciprocal effects. However, if undampened, this cumulative learning process can build enduring schemas for aggressive behavior that persist into adulthood. Thus, early childhood television habits are correlated with adult criminality independently of other likely causal factors. Therefore interventions directed at mitigating the effects of media violence on delinquency and criminality should focus on the preadolescent years. (Huesmann, 1986, p. 139)

Huesmann said the chicken and egg problem does not exist here. Rather, an interaction exists between the television viewing and the aggression: Aggression increases with viewing and viewing increases with aggression.

Other consequences stem from the response of the child's environment to aggression and from the effects of aggression on a number of intervening variables linked to both television viewing and aggression.... These variables are the child's intellectual achievement, the child's social popularity, the child's identification with television characters, the child's belief in the realism of the violence shown on television, and the child's fantasizing about aggression. (Huesmann, 1986, p. 133)

Regarding the child's intellectual achievement, Huesmann (1986) said children with poor academic skills are more aggressive and watch more television violence. More aggressive children are less popular and less popular children become more aggressive, but, in addition, the less popular children also watch more television. Some of these types of peer relationship issues have been seen in the school violence problems in places like Columbine. In addition to peer concerns, a susceptible child is one who will identify with the television characters. "Thus, aggression, violence viewing, and identification with television characters are all intercorrelated and all influence each other" (Huesmann, 1986, p. 134).

If a child also believes television violence is real, the susceptibility to violence and aggression is stronger. The last factor Huesmann listed is the child's fantasizing about aggression: "The children who report the most heroic and aggressive fantasies are those who watch a lot of television, see a lot of violence, believe the violence is realistic, and identify with television characters" (Huesmann, 1986, p. 135).

CentralXpress.com, Shades of Columbine

After the violence at Columbine High School in 1999, WRAL-TV in Raleigh, North Carolina, asked their children's program producer Dan Oliver to develop an episode based on school violence. However, Oliver had a dilemma in developing an episode for the program *CentralXpress.com* on school violence for his target audience of 11- to 14-year-olds. He knew the station management was conservative and showing any violence would be unacceptable.

The answer to his problem came from his son Josh. "'It doesn't have to be gun violence. We had a bunch of bomb threats in the schools this year,'" Oliver remembered his son saying. "They tended to come at the end of the school year because it was post Columbine and also I think if stuff like that's going to happen, it's going to tend to happen when kids are squirrelly and wanting out of school anyway," Oliver said. "And so a lot of these were coming last day of school, 'There's a rumor that on the last day of school a bomb's going to go off somewhere in Wake County.' This actually happened last year. And so he (Josh) was talking about, 'You know, we ought to do a show that just (shows) ... how the kids react to that.'"

Oliver had two goals for the show, as with many children's shows: information and entertainment. "I hope this show will be dramatically viable, but I also hope it ... has some positive effect towards lessening violence or giving people incentive to help stop the violence, even if that means showing them it's OK to be less tolerant of it," Oliver said. *CentralXpress.com* is a show about a middle school where students develop stories for their Web page. The main characters interview students and teachers on various topics that are then woven into the theme, in this case, school violence. The show has an actual Web page as well.

WRAL has had a local children's show since 1956, showing a strong commitment to children's programming even without the recent FCC requirements for educational programming. *CentralXpress.com* began in 1997 and although it is dramatic, the show also is expected to serve the educational needs of children. "It's going to have some kind of content that will both serve the audience and satisfy part of the FCC requirement," Oliver said. "Otherwise there's not a good reason for us to do it. That's the station philosophy, I think."

Eighth grader Hanna Slomianyj has been with *CentralXpress* since she was in fifth grade and describes the show as an after-school special. "Usually after-school specials have some sort of educational meaning,"

Slomianyj said. "They try and teach you a lesson and stuff. All of them pretty much have."

Seventh grader Caitlin Wells has been with the show for a few episodes and she says Columbine is important. She thinks that because *CentralXpress* is a small local show, they should tackle large issues. "If we were say a really famous show, then I would love to do fun little things, but we're not," Wells said. "And so for now, stick to the big things."

CentralXpress comes on only a few times a year, but it is distributed through the schools and is available to educators who request copies. Other shows have dealt with serious themes such as bulimia and manic depression as well as lighter things such as shopping and middle school affections.

The Bomb Scare episode aired on the first anniversary of Columbine. The main character, Shelly, promised not to tell that her friend is responsible for the bomb scare, but another friend who was innocent was being blamed. The dilemma is tough for middle-school-aged kids who are very sensitive to peer pressure. "One of the principals told us, 'We really are working hard to encourage kids to speak up if they know somebody who's bringing a handgun to school. It sounds like what we want you to do is to be an informer,'" Oliver said. "But I guess in effect it is what they want them to do. But what are they informing on? They're informing on someone who might be putting people's lives in danger, literally putting people's lives in danger." The consequences of actions, often what is missing in television programming, were made clear in Bomb Scare. "It's not cool or funny to do the bomb threat thing and in fact it has serious consequences," Oliver said.

Research on Sexuality: Schema Theory

Besides violence in the media, sexuality messages concern many adults in the audience. What children and teens bring to the sexual messages in their own experience is important to what they take away. Background knowledge plays an important role in schema theory. Being ready to learn means that the individual understands some basic aspects of the message. Brown (1993) called the schema a cognitive map. The media act as a source for adolescents in developing schema in addition to their own feelings and experiences.

> Exposure to media messages about sex also may help an individual fill in some of the gaps in a developing schema or a particular sexual script (expectations about who does what to whom in what context and for what purpose). An adolescent, for example, might not have included concern about birth control in his/her seduction script, but might begin to if (s)he saw such behavior depicted in a favorite soap opera. (Brown, 1993, p. 25)

Brown and her colleagues demonstrated with their research how the schema develops for adolescent girls at different places in their sexual development. They found all girls are not the same in their use of sexual media:

> Some find such content basically irrelevant to who they are at the time—those we called "Disinterested;" others we labeled "Intrigued" because we found them fascinated by and seeking out such content; and the third set of girls we called "Resisters," because they were less enamored with romantic fantasy the media offer and frequently were critical of how women are portrayed in sexual relationships. (Brown, White, & Nikopoulou, 1993, p. 193)

The Disinterested group was not really ready for the sexual media in their own development. The Intrigued were ready but had no personal experience. They used the sexual media to inform them and fill in information. The Resisters had some sexual experience and found the media images lacking compared to their own experiences. For these Resisters, "The reality of their own experiences did not jive with the media picture. They had begun ... to privilege their own thinking about sex and relationships and to consider relevant information from alternative media sources" (Brown et al., 1993, pp. 192–193).

Research needs to be teen-centered because it is the teen that orchestrates his or her own socialization. Only teens know why they choose the media sources they choose (Walsh-Childers & Brown, 1993).

SUMMARY

Our view of effects has come a long way from the message-based bullet theory to the more interactive presentation of Huesmann's developmental theory. Exposure to violence in mass media may continue to have effects well beyond childhood and even into the next generation. Sexual messages, like aggression messages, can become part of a child's life script as described in schema theory. The effects are complex and require attention to many variables including life experience and susceptibility. The nature of the message remains important and must provide consequences for the child to learn, not just sensational action to attract attention.

FOR FURTHER CONSIDERATION

1. Describe a child's violent or sexual act following media exposure. Choose a theory that might help to explain the act.
2. Choose a theory and draw a model that would visually depict the proposed process of this theory.
3. Which theory seems to explain effects best to your satisfaction? Why? Explain.

4. Do any of the theories presented thus far explain a media effect you have experienced or observed? Be specific in describing the effect and how the theory might apply.
5. You are assigned to a team of researchers. Your assignment is to plan an informal content analysis of the incidence of violence on television this week (beginning Sunday and ending Saturday). Your first task is to define what they are looking for. How do you define violence? What are areas of difficulty you might encounter? The scribe in your group will distribute the definition of violence and some of the guidelines you come up with in your plan. Suggestions: Violence definitions may depend on what type of program it is. Also, you may consider motivation. Why is the person committing violence? In your English class, this might be called *narrative function*. Another variable might be the artistic value. Is violence acceptable if it is in Shakespeare? The Bible? (Davies, 1997). Report back to the class how you defined violence and the difficulties you anticipated.
6. Obesity also has been shown to be an effect of media use as in the Toles cartoon Figure 5.3. Find evidence that supports the hypothesis that obesity can be an effect of media use. Report your findings to the class.

FIG. 5.3.   Obesity has been linked to media use. TOLES © The Buffalo News. Reprinted by permission of UNIVERSAL PRESS SYNDICATE. All rights reserved.

REFERENCES

Ashby, H. (Director). (1979). *Being there* [Motion picture]. United States: Warner Studios.

Brown, J. D. (1993). Theoretical view. In B. S. Greenberg, J. D. Brown, & N. Buerkel- Rothfuss (Eds.), *Media, sex and the adolescent* (pp. 19–25). Cresskill, NJ: Hampton.

Brown, J. D., White, A. B., & Nikopoulou, L. (1993). Disinterest, intrigue, resistance: Early adolescent girls' use of sexual media content. In B. S. Greenberg, J. D. Brown, & N. Buerkel-Rothfuss (Eds.), *Media, sex and the adolescent* (pp. 177–195). Cresskill, NJ: Hampton.

Cooper, C. (1996). *Violence on television, Congressional inquiry, public criticism and industry response: A policy analysis.* Lanham, MD: University Press of America.

Davies, M. M. (1997). Making media literate: Educating future media workers at the undergraduate level. In R. Kubey (Ed.), *Media literacy in the information age, current perspectives, information and behavior* (Vol. 6, pp. 263–284). New Brunswick, NJ: Transaction.

Eron, L. D., & Huesmann, L. R. (1984). The control of aggressive behavior by changes in attitudes, values, and the conditions of learning. In R. J. Blanchard & D. C. Blanchard (Eds.), *Advances in the study of aggression* (Vol. 1, pp. 139–171). Orlando, FL: Academic.

Heller, J. (1982). TV new for teens. In M. Schwartz (Ed.), *TV & teens: Experts look at the issues* (pp. 31–34). Reading, MA: Addison-Wesley.

Huesmann, L. R. (1986). Psychological processes promoting the relation between exposure to media violence and aggressive behavior by the viewer. *Journal of Social Issues, 42,* 125–139.

Huston, A. C., Donnerstein, E., Fairchild, H., Feshbach, N. D., Katz, P., Murray, J. P., et al. (1992). *Big world, small screen: The role of television in American society.* Lincoln: University of Nebraska Press.

Kosinski, J. (1970). *Being there.* New York: Harcourt, Brace Jovanovich.

Macbeth, T. M. (1996). Introduction. In T. M. Macbeth (Ed.), *Tuning in to young viewers, social science perspectives on television* (pp. 1–35). Thousand Oaks, CA: Sage.

Schramm, W., Lyle, J., & Parker E. B. (1961). *Television in the lives of our children.* Stanford, CA: Stanford University Press.

Singer, J. (1982). Introductory comments to cognitive and affective aspects of television. In D. Pearl, L. Bouthilet, & J. Lazar (Eds.), *Television and behavior: Ten years of scientific progress and implications for the eighties.* Vol. II. *Technical reviews* (pp. 2–8). Washington, DC: U.S. Department of Health and Human Services and National Institute of Mental Health.

Strasburger, V. C. (1995). *Adolescents and the media, medical and psychological impact.* Thousand Oaks, CA: Sage.

Strouse, J. S., & Buerkel-Rothfuss, N. L. (1993). Media exposure and the sexual attitudes and behaviors of college students. In B. S. Greenberg, J. D. Brown, & N. Buerkel-Rothfuss (Eds.), *Media, sex and the adolescent* (pp. 277–292). Cresskill, NJ: Hampton.

U.S. Department of Health and Human Services. (2001). *Youth violence: A report of the Surgeon General.* Rockville, MD: U.S. Department of Health and Human Services, Centers for Disease Control and Prevention, National Center for Injury Prevention and Control, Substance Abuse and Mental Health Services Administration, Center for Mental Health Services, and National Institutes of Health, National Institute of Mental Health.

U.S. Surgeon General's Scientific Advisory Committee on Television and Social Behavior. (1972). *Television and growing up: The impact of television violence; Report of the Surgeon General.* (HE 20: T23). Washington, DC: U.S. Government Printing Office.

Walsh-Childers, K., & Brown, J. D. (1993). Adolescents' acceptance of sex-role stereotypes and television viewing. In B. S. Greenberg, J. D. Brown, & N. Buerkel-Rothfuss (Eds.), *Media, sex and the adolescent* (pp. 117–133). Cresskill, NJ: Hampton.

Williams, T. M. (1986). *The impact of television: A natural experiment in three communities.* New York: Academic.

Wilson, B. J., Kunkel, D., Linz, D., Potter, J., Donnerstein, E., Smith, S., et al. (1998). Violence in television programming overall: University of California, Santa Barbara study. In M. Seawall (Ed), *National television violence study* (Vol. 2, pp. 3–204). Thousand Oaks, CA: Sage.

CHAPTER SIX

Diverse Children Find Identity in Diverse Messages

To compare perceptions between Anglos and Native Americans, Highwater (1982) asked an Indian to draw the scene of the arrival of Columbus in 1492 (see Fig. 6.1) and asked Anglos and Native Americans to compare the Indian drawing to a 16th-century etching done by a European. This describes the scene painted by an Indian:

> ... three Indians crouched on the shore, staring in amazement at the water, where a floating island of rock was gradually approaching. The island was covered with tall defoliated trees in which vines and various leaves seemed to be blowing in the wind. Beneath them were strange men wrapped in some peculiar kind of shell, who looked as if they had squirrels in their mouths, they were so bushy.
>
> I showed these two pictures to a group of Indians and a group of non-Indians, and the Anglos said, "Well, if you think about it, the Indians really didn't see what they thought they saw. The island is really a ship and those defoliated trees are really masts, and those people had beards; there weren't squirrels in their mouths. They simply didn't know what they were looking at, so they made an error." The Indians looked at them for a long time and then said, "After all, isn't the ship really a floating island, and what are the masts finally, but tall defoliated trees?" We see reality in terms of the way in which we experience it. (p. 100)

Children's self-identity by ethnicity, among other things, is affected by their experiences, including their observations of mass media images. What they see in the mass media among other experiences affects their idea of who they are as well as how they perceive the world. Although the effects of violent and sexual images may grab our immediate attention, it is children's self-identity and its development that has long-term effects. "This accumulated experience contributes to the cultivation of a child's values, beliefs, dreams, and expectations, which shape the adult identity a child will carry and modify throughout his or her life" (Huntemann & Morgan, 2001, p. 311).

FIG. 6.1.   Individuals from diverse backgrounds may perceive the same event differently. Matt Tacy, age 10, illustrates the arrival of Columbus with an Indian looking on.
Reprinted with permission.

Mass media may provide images for children and teens that they do not
encounter in their daily lives and thus provide them with an introduction to
groups they may have little contact with in their own experience. On the other
hand, mass media can provide narrow stereotypes that limit views of certain
groups in our culture.

We form impressions of a particular group based on our experiences with individual representatives of that group. If we are exposed to relatively few individuals or to

individuals in relatively few roles, we have little choice but to form limited stereotypes and to rely on these stereotypes. On the other hand, if we are exposed to numerous individuals who represent a particular group, and these individuals are seen in a wide variety of roles, stereotypes break down, and we have more opportunity to identify areas of commonality between ourselves and them. (Makas, 1993, p. 256)

In addition, mass media images may tend to depict various myths about stereotyped groups and their identity by gender, race, or association with the products of consumer culture.

LEARNING THEORY AND SCHEMA THEORY

One theory we use to help explain children's responses to the messages we examine is learning theory (see chapter 1). Simply put, learning theory predicts that "Positive information leads to positive stereotypes; negative information leads to negative stereotypes" (Tan, Fujioka, & Lucht, 1997, p. 270). "Stereotypes are overgeneralizations that constitute denial of individual differences among racial and other 'out' groups" (Tan et al., 1997, p. 265). The media provide us with shared understandings. "Since the media influence how people treat us, as clusters of demographic and cultural characteristics, social interactions are in part informed by the shared understandings or stereotypes about people that the media provide" (Huntemann & Morgan, 2001, p. 311).

Stereotypes in turn affect the child's development of self-identity. Children add to their immediate environment with media and then talk about those additional media experiences. The influences of the media on identity vary by age and developmental level and by individual. Greenberg and Atkin (1982) provided a model for social learning based on learning theory. The model includes peer and family variables, child viewer variables, and message variables. The child viewer variables combined with the content affect and are affected by exposure, interpretation, and effects. The peer and family variables affect child viewer characteristics and produce viewing patterns and discussions that impact exposure and interpretation (p. 235).

In addition to learning theory, schema theory helps to explain the development of identity. The media images contribute to the development of schema by youth at different ages (Huntemann & Morgan, 2001):

A viewer, for example, may learn the social definition of what it means to be a young black female or a working-class white male. Moreover, these elements may guide our schemas and expectations in dealing with different types of people, which may then indirectly contribute to others' sense of identity. (p. 312)

The schemata are important to the development of self-identity. "Beyond the more typical socializing role, television teaches ethnic minority children subtle lessons about themselves and how they are perceived. The portrayals are sparse and almost uniformly negative" (Palmer, Smith, & Strawser, 1993, p. 144). The underrepresentation of many minorities is problematic. Cultural minorities and children use the mass media as a tool of acculturation. "Mass media play an important role in providing information to those new to a cultural environment" (Taylor & Bang, 1997, p. 287). The dominant culture may communicate by under-representation of groups in mass media "messages of indifference or lack of acceptance of minorities by the majority" (p. 287).

THE DEVELOPMENT OF ETHNIC MINORITY MASS MEDIA IMAGES

Minority depictions show the identity of the group portrayed and may lead to observational learning for children in the audience who are like the characters as well as those who are different. The process by which minority depictions in the mass media seem to develop over time can be illustrated in four steps.

1. No Depictions or Few Depictions: Native Americans

At first, there are no depictions or few depictions. Gross (1995) called the lack of images "symbolic annihilation" (pp. 62–63). The Native American is perhaps the least visible minority in the United States. The Native Americans include American Indians, Eskimos, and Aleuts (Alaska Natives; Tan et al., 1997). However, Tan and his colleagues asked their research participants to provide the images instead of looking at the numbers of images. They focused their research on the audience and their way of viewing the message. They also found that of the theories they tried to use to interpret their research, learning theory seemed to best explain their results. Learning theory works well in a situation with fewer images because it looks at the degree of attractiveness or valence rather than quantity of information. Tan et al. asked what predicted the stereotyping that their group of research participants had:

> Our study shows that two variables consistently predicted stereotyping of Native American by white college students: frequency of personal contact and evaluation of first contact. Frequent personal contact led to positive stereotyping as did positive evaluations of first contact (more so than positive evaluations of contact in general). These findings support a learning theory interpretation of stereotyping.... We suspect that the key variable is evaluation of first contact, and that the direction of influence is from evaluation of first contact to frequency of personal contact to stereotyping. (pp. 279–280)

Thus Tan et al. attributed the stereotyping to the individual and interactions with the subject being stereotyped.

2. Negative Images: Evil and Bad Guys

The connection of evil and minority depictions goes back to the idea of the enemy who must be dehumanized to justify killing in war or unequal treatment. Childhood stories include a disability that disappears if one is virtuous or patient. Examples include Pinocchio's nose that grew when he lied, the ugly duckling that turned into a swan, and Beast who turned into Beauty's prince. Children's programming also has used disabilities to create situations that are humorous, as with Porky Pig's stuttering, Elmer Fudd's speech impairment, Mr. McGoo's nearsightedness, and Dopey's mental retardation (Makas, 1993). Public television programs such as *Sesame Street* consistently have presented people of color and people with disabilities. *Sesame Street* uses both segments that talk about the disability and segments in which there is no attention brought to the disability. More programming for children and adults now presents persons with disabilities as simply one of the characters.

Greenberg and Collette (1997) reported from their research of characters in fall season premieres that 10% of the characters in their content analysis were African American. They looked at 27 fall seasons and noted "a steady upward trend toward increased new black characters" (p. 8). The trend became strong in the mid-1980s: "Beginning in 1984, percentages ranged from 10% (1987) to 24%, with an average of 15% of all new characters being black" (p. 8).

FIG. 6.2. Negative depictions of people in crime shows, as illustrated by Kelty McGonagle, age 10, may lead to stereotypes. Reprinted with permission.

Although the numbers may increase, negative depictions may be part of that increase, based on the majority's prejudices and the political climate. In some cases the negative depictions are very popular with the majority, perhaps because the depictions reinforce stereotypes.

The depictions of the "bad guys" in crime shows illustrate a negative effect of stereotyping. Where races do appear in the same shows, differences are based on race. Research on reality-based police shows, for example, shows that "non-whites are typically the 'bad guys'" (Oliver, 1994, p. 190).

> These programs tend to underrepresent blacks and overrepresent whites as police officers in comparison to government statistics (U.S. Department of Labor Statistics, 1992). Although criminal suspects are generally not overrepresented as racial minorities in comparison with FBI reports (U.S. Department of Justice, 1991), these programs are much more likely to portray whites as police officers (or heroes) and non-whites as criminal suspects (for villains).... In addition, black and Hispanic criminal suspects are significantly more likely than white criminal suspects to suffer from unarmed physical aggression from police officers. (Oliver, 1994, p. 189)

Racial depictions in entertainment thus could both reinforce stereotypes and suggest biases in the popular genre of crime shows.

Minority children in particular are affected by these negative images.

> Prolonged exposure to these stereotypical images inhibits minority children's interest in wanting to be a part of the larger, host society. The end result is a twofold tragedy. On the one hand, these children and their families experience a lowered self-concept. On the other, these same children grow up separate and apart. The television tool through which they sought socialization and integration in the final analysis separates them. (Palmer et al., 1993, pp. 144–145)

The separation of ethnic groups can be seen in the next part of the development of images, images that are segregated as single ethnic group portrayals.

3. Single Ethnic Group Portrayals: African Americans

When the negative stereotypes are challenged, the process continues with more positive images in a single program series, often based on humor. Research indicates that in our mass media of the 1980s particularly, segregation can be seen by race. Where we do see people of color, we see them together. However, sometimes these narrow stereotypes lead to challenges as well. A 1970s television example is *Good Times*, which star Esther Rolle quit because of the stereotype of the character J.J.

In the United States, although the most represented minority group is African Americans, those representations fall short in message quality and numbers.

Graves (1993) reported "minorities ... are underrepresented on TV, segregated in specific types of content, and rarely engage in cross-ethnic interactions" (p. 179).

> Diverse characters that are shown are restricted to specific content ghettos. When visible racial-ethnic groups are portrayed, they are restricted in terms of their roles, occupations, and personality characteristics. The limited roles and scope of action assigned to visible racial-ethnic groups reduces chances for diverse people to en- counter one another. (Graves, 1996, pp. 71–72)

The content ghettos, however sometimes can also illustrate the ethnic group in glowing terms as seen in *The Cosby Show*.

Portrayals that reflect majority culture may follow negative content ghettos. Those who have mainstreamed into the dominant culture, such as Bill Cosby, can make race seem irrelevant when the other variables such as profession and family structure reflect the dominant culture. Besides Cosby, another depiction might be the Jeffersons "moving on up to the East Side."

The 1980s witnessed the beginning of *The Cosby Show*. "The series proved that a program about a Black American created and produced by a Black American could be economically successful and popular with the mainstream broadcast television audience without resorting to traditional Black stereotypes and depreciating hu- mor" (Tucker, 1997, p. 90). However, all the research on *The Cosby Show* was not pos- itive. *The Cosby Show* was also criticized for not representing the diversity of African American life and the middle-class lifestyle of the Huxtables that seemed more typi- cal of White than Black families. However, some research has shown that African American youth perceived *The Cosby Show* characters as true to life (Graves, 1993). Perhaps the most important effect for African American children is in self-esteem ef- fects and self-concept. However, there is no conclusive evidence that television can influence the self-concept of African American children (Graves, 1993).

The impact of African American portrayals on other ethnic American children seems to be more consistent in providing evidence that exposure to these portrayals improves cross-group attitudes, particularly if the depiction is positive. Studies show that viewing *Sesame Street*, for example, is associated with positive racial attitudes, whereas viewing violent programming is related to negative racial stereotypes. It must be noted, however, that studies also show that children who have personal contact with other ethnic groups are less susceptible to television depictions because they have their own experience to inform their decisions about reality (Graves, 1993).

4. Variety of Depictions

Finally a variety of depictions with a variety of images more reflective of reality seem to emerge. Differences are ignored in integrated ensemble casts where little reference is made to racial differences. In public television children's shows, ensemble casts have been dominant since *Sesame Street* and have continued with programs such as *Ghost Writer.*

Although Latino Americans are underrepresented in U.S. English media, Spanish-language media provide many other images. Latino American depictions on mainstream U.S. television were under 1% in a population of 27 television seasons studied. Of those, only "13 Hispanics could be identified as having major roles" (Greenberg & Collette, 1997, p. 8). Latino Americans have been defined in some research as "Mexican Americans, Cuban Americans, Puerto Ricans, and other Latinos who immigrated to the United States from Central and South America or Spain" (Taylor & Bang, 1997, p. 291). Latino American depictions may suffer lower numbers in mainstream media in part because there are other sources.

There are two other television worlds for Latino Americans besides the U.S. media in English. U.S. Spanish-language television programs began in

> 1951 when Jose Perez del Rio, a Mexican national of Spanish heritage, hosted a weekly entertainment and variety talent search show that was broadcast live on Sunday afternoons from the studio of KERN Channel 5, an English-language station in San Antonio, Texas. (Subervi-Velez & Colsant, 1993, p. 220)

Today there are at least three such networks including Univision (founded in 1961), Telemundo (founded in 1987) and Galavision (founded in 1979). Children's programs on Spanish-language TV "regularly feature Spanish-speaking, Latino-type characters, studio participants, and role models" (Subervi-Velez & Colsant, 1993, p. 224).

The third television world is Spanish-language programming originating in Spanish-speaking countries, the "'home' country or country of their ancestors" (Subervi-Velez & Colsant, 1993, p. 225).

The preceding process is not necessarily linear. There have been periods of improved numbers and images followed by underrepresentation, as in the fall 1999 season of programs, which were criticized for their lack of minority representation of people of color.

Not only are the images harmful, but they also are false and do not reflect cultural reality. In television content analyses over the years, the characters on TV have been found generally to be White adult males with a professional, high-income job, and they are no older than middle age. The TV characters do not reflect the demographics of the culture. "Despite increases in the number of minority characters, the depictions of minorities have generally not been aligned with population figures.... Minorities, including Blacks, Asians and American Indians, comprised less than five percent of the characters on TV" (Greenberg & Collette, 1997, p. 3). Thus the images children see on television are the dominant culture's race.

CHILDREN'S IDENTITY AND GENDER

In addition to ethnicity, children's identity development includes gender, and during adolescence identity development includes sex roles. "Identity—teens' sense of themselves and others—affects the media they like best, how they interact with that media, and how they apply media matter in their everyday lives" (Steele, 1999, paragraph 1). Teens' gender makes a difference in which media they select. One study shows that African American teen girls' music preference differs from that of African American boys as well as from that of White girls.

> Black artists or musical groups such as Mary J. Blige, Brandi, and Salt 'N' Pepa were listed by several of the Black females, but none of the Black males. Similarly, White musicians were not listed as boys' favorites, only girls'. Gender crossovers were more frequent with television shows. (Results, Identity and Lived Experience, paragraph 11)

Although boys and girls may choose different media, both boys and girls suffer negative effects in self-esteem if they buy into media images. Polce-Lynch, Myers, Kliewer, and Kilmartin (2001) looked at students in Grades 5, 8, and 12 regarding their self-esteem and the media. Like other studies, this one found evidence that teens have less self-esteem if they accept media messages about appearance:

> The acceptance of media messages (in television, advertisements, movies) about the importance of physical appearance is negatively related to general feelings about the self. This was true for boys and girls in each age group, except early adolescent boys.... The influence of media played a unique role for girls in that media messages were associated with body image, which in turn was negatively associated with self-esteem. (p. 239)

Although girls and boys both are affected, the emphasis for girls is on physical appearance, and they are underrepresented.

The gender story is similar to ethnic depictions with underrepresentation of women. In their study of new shows for each fall season from 1966 through 1994, Greenberg and Collette (1997) found "the population was almost two-thirds male (65%, 1,142) and one-third female (35%, 615) reflecting a true gender gap in presentation of new characters throughout the 27 seasons" (p. 6). The one third proportion falls short of the more than 50% of the population women account for. Even then the one third proportion was not consistently present until 1983. As with ethnic depictions, gender depictions were stereotyped:

> In general, female characters make more limited appearances on television than do males, are more likely to be portrayed in stereotyped fashion, and are portrayed as considerable younger.... Females are more likely to be limited to supporting roles, and even those female characters simply do not exist to the same degree as males.... Where numbers of female characters were found to increase through time, they still remain consistently far below that of their male counterparts.... The disparity in roles is reduced only when television soaps are considered as females have nearly half of those roles. (pp. 2–3)

For boys, the images support a long-standing "boy code" that keeps boys from their true selves.

> The boys we care for, much like the girls we cherish, often seem to feel they must live semi-authentic lives, lives that conceal much of their true selves and feelings, and studies show they do so in order to fit in and be loved. (Pollack, 1998, p. 7)

The boy code Pollack (1998) talked about is a stereotype that traps boys. It includes images we find in the media: "The four basic stereotyped, male ideals or models of behavior ... are at the heart of the Boy Code" (p. 23). The boys code includes "The 'sturdy oak,'" model, the "'Give 'em hell'" model, the "'Big Wheel'" model and the "'No sissy stuff'" model (Pollack, 1998, pp. 23–24). The "sturdy oak" model says even boys should not show weakness. Even when women are in men's roles they are expected to go by this ideal. For example, in the movie *A League of Their Own*, the coach played by Tom Hanks tells the female baseball players, "There's no crying in baseball." A second model is "Give 'em hell" as seen in roles showing daring beyond the norms of society. An example of this type of character in children's books might be Harry Potter. A third model is the "Big Wheel," where boys must avoid shame and be very cool even when things are out of control. Finally, there is the "No sissy stuff" ideal epitomized by the saying "You throw like a girl." Inspirational speaker and former professional football quarterback Don McPherson uses that phrase to explain to young people the dangers of men losing touch with their feminine side. McPherson describes this part of the boy code as a box that men retreat into when they are accused of being in touch with their female side.

RESULTS OF GENDER IMAGES IN ADVERTISING AND MEDIA

The models for male and female behavior have been in society for a long time. However, research has shown that these images in the mass media may have some effects. Kilbourne (1982) saw objectification as the result of advertising depictions of males and females: "Women, especially young women, are primarily depicted as sex objects and men as success objects. In both cases, the person becomes a thing, and his or her value depends upon the products used" (p. 212).

Huston and Alvarez (1990) summarized the literature on the topic of influence of the sex-typed images on attitudes: "Most television presents highly stereotyped images of adult men and women and both longitudinal and experimental studies support the hypothesis that televised sex roles influence children's sex stereotypes and attitudes. The evidence for effects on behavior is weaker than that for attitudes" (p.173). Although a content analysis with its focus on the message cannot prove negative images have negative effects on children and teen viewers, learning theory indicates that negative attitudes can develop.

Signorielli, McLeod, and Healy (1994) described MTV commercials as including more than twice the number of males than females, with males more likely than females to control objects being advertised and product types for females being personal enhancement products versus entertainment products for males .

> If adolescents, as is likely, utilize MTV as a source of social learning about gender roles, then they receive warped views of the roles and responsibilities of women in society. While we cannot say there is a causal relationship between commercial content and social problems like rape, eating disorders, and discrimination in the workplace, MTV commercials in no way contribute to a reduction of misconceptions about women and women's roles in society. (Signorielli et al., 1994, pp. 99–100)

The music videos themselves also can influence gender identification. Tapper, Thorson, and Black (1994) identified music video genres as rap, soul, country, heavy metal, pop, classic rock, and alternative rock for music videos in 1992. One observation that applied to all music videos is the domination of male lead performers: "The heaviest concentration of white male lead performers was in the classic rock genre. Soul had the heaviest concentration of female lead performers" (p. 108). As might be expected, rap and soul music videos appeared most often on Black Entertainment Television and starred Black males or females. Minorities appeared in all videos in the rap and soul genres. The rap music videos also appeared on MTV. In contrast, heavy metal videos appeared most often on MTV, with some on VH-1. "Almost all lead performers in this genre were white males and minorities rarely appeared in the videos of this musical genre" (pp. 111–112).

Music itself has been a way for groups to develop identities. In looking at radio audiences (specifically college students), Edwards and Singletary (1989) found that "radio audiences constitute subcultures whose members actively use radio music in developing or validating personal identity" (p. 155). Some researchers have gone so far as to attribute ethnic identity to music. Specifically, "free jazz as a style of music helped to develop the self-image and cultural identity of the black American community, aligning black Americans with Third World peoples" (p. 149).

Eating disorders also have been linked to media consumption for adolescents. The research on the relationship of eating disorders and media use does not conclusively prove any causal relationship, but some research has provided some conclusions about the correlation between eating disorders and media: "There is evidence that adolescent girls' images of their own bodies are influenced by the mass media's portrayal of ideal body types" (Harrison & Cantor, 1997, p. 43). Learning theory has been supported in some studies that find relationships between media consumption and eating disorders for college-age students. "Respondents' eating disorder symptomatology was significantly related to media consumption, especially TDP (thinness-depicting, thinness-promoting) media" (Harrison & Cantor, 1997, p. 64) The symptoms referred to include body dissatisfaction and drive for thinness. However, it is interesting to note that magazines, not television, seem to have the strongest relationship to eating disorders. Researchers explain that because television encourages the consumption of high-fat foods, the effect toward eating disorders is minimized. On the other hand, magazines offer more instruction on dieting and therefore seem to be more significantly correlated to eating disorders.

Adolescent girls may be vulnerable to the negative effects of MTV ads, but younger children are more likely than older teens to be open to gender equity ideas. Studies done on models of women scientists show that the early years are the most important for establishing the possibility that a girl will consider science as a career:

> Gender schema theory suggests that creating gender schemata that are free of gender role stereotypes of science during the early years of development may be more effective than altering existing, stereotyped gender schemata. Exposing preschool-aged girls to female characters portrayed as scientists on television programs like *Sesame Street*, for example, might be more effective in teaching girls that science is an appropriate career for women than exposing adolescent girls to women scientists on series like *Discovering Women*. (Steinke, 1998, p. 148).

Ads in children's programs also have women underrepresented. Riffe, Goldson, Saxton, and Yu (1989) found that although the number of females and people of color increased from the 1970s to the late 1980s, "the world of children's television advertising remains predominantly male and white" (p. 136).

Later research looked at single gender characters in children's advertising and found that in gender-neutral products boys were exclusively used instead of girls. However, contrary to earlier findings, girls were not restricted to passive activities in the girls-only ads. Stereotypical behaviors did predominate, however: "Only boys performed antisocial actions in ads. They were the mischief-makers, the ones evading the law and making trouble for their parents. Girls did not challenge authority; they respected their parents and cooperated rather than competing with one another" (Smith, 1994, p. 334). Smith (1994) found that the setting of the ads for the single gender characters was the most stereotyped. For boys, away-from-home settings were the most prevalent, but girls were in the home setting more than 70% of the time. Smith concluded that the depictions of boys are also problematic because boys are not depicted as nurturing or sharing.

Some researchers have studied programming and the depicted consequences of behaviors. Barner (1999) looked at educational television in the summer of 1997 and found ensemble casts, but none with a female central character. He looked for female behaviors with consequence but found few:

> The lack of consequences given to females in this sample is not surprising considering the behaviors they tend to exhibit. Male behaviors such as construction,

dominance, and attention seeking are more likely to command some consequence whether it is positive or negative. For example, if someone makes a plan,
they either carry it out or do not; if someone seeks attention, they either get it or
they do not. Behaviors such as deference, dependence, and nurturance, however,
do not warrant such consequences. The fact that female characters tend to exhibit
these behaviors means that they are not given the power to get results through
their social behaviors. They are relegated to behaviors which, by their very nature,
warrant no consequence. In effect, females are ignored and remain powerless because of it …

Specifically, if a young girl sees her favorite female TV character continually ignored
for their actions, she is probably less likely to expect consequences to her own
actions and less likely to question their absence. In this way, sex-role stereotyping in
children's television programs may help naturalize acceptable (and unacceptable)
gendered behaviors in real life. (Barner, 1999, pp. 561–562)

Perhaps looking for consequences, by definition, excludes girls. However,
television itself leaves out consequences of many behaviors for both boys and
girls. The consequences of violence, for example, often are not shown. In
children's cartoons, characters often are violently treated and yet do not die or
experience much in terms of consequence at all. Consequences of negative
behaviors such as drinking and smoking are other examples of areas where the
mass media have left out consequences to the detriment of the truthfulness of the
messages.

However, the conclusion that the same images have differing consequences for
boys and girls is apparent. The more powerful position of men in society is
reinforced by the images on television and in other mass media.

Our results suggest that boys' and girls' TV consumption has different consequences, strengthening boys' self-image while inhibiting that of girls. An explanation of these gender differences is that through the socialization process girls
become increasingly aware of men's greater power and higher prestige in society
compared to women. Girls also meet appreciation for their very lack of independ-
ence and lack of self-assertion. This gender-specific socialization tends to encourage girls to a more self-critical attitude towards themselves. Thus, low self-esteem is
a means for girls to be obedient to the cultural expectations of society, thus arriving
at a measure of success. (Johnsson-Smaragdi & Jonsson, 1994, p. 178)

Both boys and girls see the same images, but boys have their tangible "success"
supported and girls are rewarded more for being self-critical and successful in the
nontangible areas of nurturing and caring.

In postmodernist society, the very definition of gender is being questioned. In
an essay on the TV show *Xena, Warrior Princess*, Morreale (1998) used feminist
theory to analyze the TV program:

Moments in the text where femininity is reenacted underscore femininity as construction rather than essence. In the more specific case of the beauty pageant parodied in *Xena* we are shown the absurdity of women's status as spectacle. Mimickry and parody become politicized textual strategies. It is in this sense that we may regard *Xena* as a feminist text, one that enables viewers to perceive the artifice of both masculinity and femininity. (p. 86)

Morreale (1998) explained that Xena (*stranger* in Greek) is a hero on a quest, but when she enters the beauty pageant, she is putting on a more traditional woman's image, or "spectacle." As a strong woman, Xena must mimic the traditional woman's role in the beauty pageant and thus parodies the pageant. These images can break down the images we have of femininity and make us realize that they are human creations.

CHILDREN AND CONSUMER SOCIALIZATION

Identity development can also be seen as children seeing themselves as consumers. Socialization to cultural norms as seen in programming is more focused in advertising where socialization is aimed at consumer roles: "Consumer socialization is the developmental process by which young people acquire the knowledge, attitudes, and skills relevant to their functioning in the marketplace" (Atkin, 1982, p. 191). Consumer socialization is focused on the specific response of buying a product. The research shows that product preference is affected particularly for those children who are heavy viewers of television. Not only are brand preferences encouraged by exposure to advertising, but general consumption is stimulated as well (Atkin, 1982).

If we look at the messages in the mass media, we see an emphasis on materialism. "Wealth and occupations that promise increased earning power have been over-represented on television" (Greenberg & Collette, 1997, p. 4):

The most represented occupations, nearly one quarter of the characters ($N = 419$, 24%), were professionals (doctor, lawyer, accountant).... (Twelve percent) were children/students, 9% were blue collar laborers such as factory workers or ranch hands, 5% were craftspersons.... As for occupation and gender, 27% of all males and 17% of females were professionals.... More females were home care workers and unskilled laborers than males. (p. 9)

The economic position of demographic groups may be an important depiction for youth to experience in the mass media.

As a generational issue, the youngest always are the most "hip," according to Frank (1997) in his book, *The Conquest of Cool: Business Culture, Counterculture, and the Rise of Hip Consumerism*. What advertisers realized during the 1960s was that the counterculture attitude of the baby boomers was exactly the type of attitude that would free consumers to buy whatever was the newest because they were not restricted by religious puritanism or by conformity. "Admen believed they had found an entire generation given over to self-fulfillment by whatever means necessary—which would, of course, ultimately mean by shopping" (Frank, 1997, pp. 121–122). The counterculture of the 1960s gave the advertisers a new icon of the cultural rebel:

> Whether he is an athlete decked out in a mohawk and multiple-pierced ears, a po-liceman who plays by his own rules, an actor on a motorcycle, a movie fratboy wreaking havoc on the townies' parade, a soldier of fortune with explosive bow and arrow, a long-haired alienated cowboy gunning down square cowboys, or a rock star in leather jacket and sunglasses, he has become the paramount cliché of our popular entertainment, the preeminent symbol of the system he is supposed to be subverting. In advertising, especially, he rules supreme. (Frank, 1997, pp. 227–228)

The youth of the 1960s gave way to the youth of succeeding generations and the younger always were more "hip" than the older ones. The medium of television itself became the means of mocking authority. Because television gets the approval of the audience by mocking authority, it becomes the only authority, according to Frank (1997).

SUMMARY

In conclusion, the images we see in the media seem to be intentional. They support the status quo power by perpetuating the myths of our culture beginning with the very young. The intentionality of this process is not new. It began with the earliest socialization of children into society and has been refined with mass media use.

RESOURCES ON THE WEB

* http://www.jeankilbourne.com

REFERENCES

Atkin, C. K. (1982). Television advertising and socialization to consumer roles. In D. Pearl, L. Bouthilet, & J. Lazar (Eds.), *Television and behavior: Ten years of scientific progress and implications for the eighties. Vol. II. Technical reviews* (pp. 191–200). Washington, DC: U.S. Department of Health and Human Services and National Institute of Mental Health.

Barner, M. R. (1999). Sex-role stereotyping in FCC-mandated children's educational television. *Journal of Broadcasting and the Electronic Media, 43,* 551–564.

Edwards, E. D., & Singletary, M. W. (1989, Winter). Life's soundtracks: Relationships between radio music subcultures and listeners' belief systems. *The Southern Communication Journal, 54,* 144–158.

Frank, T. (1997). *The conquest of cool: Business culture, counterculture, and the rise of hip consumerism.* Chicago: University of Chicago Press.

Graves, S. B. (1993). Television, the portrayal of African Americans, and the development of children's attitudes. In G. L. Berry & J. K. Asamen (Eds.), *Children and television: Images in a changing sociocultural world* (pp. 179–190). Newbury Park, CA: Sage.

Graves, S. B. (1996). Diversity on television. In T. M. Macbeth (Ed.), *Tuning in to young viewers: Social science perspectives on television* (pp. 61–83). Thousand Oaks, CA: Sage.

Greenberg, B. S., & Atkin, C. K. (1982). Learning about minorities from television: A research agenda. In G. L. Berry & C. Mitchell-Kernan (Eds.), *Television and the socialization of the minority child* (pp. 215–243). New York: Academic.

Greenberg, B. S., & Collette, L. (1997, Winter). The changing faces on TV: A demographic analysis of network television's new seasons, 1966–1992. *Journal of Broadcasting and the Electronic Media, 41,* 1–13.

Gross, L. (1995). Out of the mainstream, sexual minorities and the media. In G. Dines, Gail & J. M. Humez (Eds.), *Gender, race and class in media: A text-reader* (pp. 61–69). Thousand Oaks, CA: Sage.

Harrison, K., & Cantor, J. (1997, Winter). The relationship between media consumption and eating disorders. *Journal of Communication, 47,* 40–67.

Highwater, J. (1982). Minority role models, Native Americans. In M. Schwartz (Ed.), *TV & teens: Experts look at the issues* (pp. 96–100). Reading, MA: Addison-Wesley.

Huntemann, N., & Morgan, M. (2001). Mass media and identity development. In D. G. Singer & J. L. Singer (Eds.), *Handbook of children and the media* (pp. 309–322). Thousand Oaks, CA: Sage.

Huston, A. C., & Alvarez, M. M. (1990). The socialization context of gender role development in early adolescence. In G. R. Adams, R. Montemayor, & T. P. Gullotta (Series Eds.) & R. Montemayor, G. R. Adams, & T. P. Gullotta (Vol. Eds.), *Advances in adolescent development: Vol. 2. From childhood to adolescence: A transitional period?* (pp. 156–179). Newbury Park, CA: Sage.

Johnsson-Smaragdi, U., & Jonsson, A. (1994). Self-evaluation in an ecological perspective: Neighbourhood, family and peers, schooling and media use. In K. E. Rosengren (Vol. Ed.) & J. Curran (Gen. Ed.), *Media effects and beyond: Culture, socialization and lifestyles* (pp. 150–182). London: Routledge.

Kilbourne, J. (1982). Sex roles in advertising. In M. Schwartz (Ed.), *TV & teens: Experts look at the issues* (pp. 211–216). Reading, MA: Addison-Wesley.

Makas, E. (1993). Changing channels: The portrayal of people with disabilities on television. In G. L. Berry, J. K. Asamen, & J. Keiko (Eds.), *Children and television: Images in a changing sociocultural world* (pp. 255–268). Newbury Park, CA: Sage.

Morreale, J. (1998, Fall). Xena: Warrior princess as feminist camp. *Journal of Popular Culture, 32,* 79–86.

Oliver, M. B. (1994, Spring). Portrayals of crime, race, and aggression in "reality-based" police shows: A content analysis. *Journal of Broadcasting and Electronic Media, 38,* 179–192.

Palmer, E. L., Smith, K. T., & Strawser, K. S. (1993). Rubik's tube: Developing a child's television worldview. In G. L. Berry & J. K. Asamen (Eds.), *Children and television: Images in a changing sociocultural world* (pp. 143–154). Newbury Park, CA: Sage.

Polce-Lynch, M., Myers, B. J., Kliewer, W., & Kilmartin, C. (2001). Adolescent self-esteem and gender: Exploring relations to sexual harassment, body image, media influence, and emotional expression [Electronic version]. *Journal of Youth and Adolescence, 30,* 225–244.

Pollack, W. (1998). *Real boys: Rescuing our sons from the myths of boyhood.* New York: Holt.

Riffe, D., Goldson, H., Saxton, K., & Yu, Y. (1989, Spring). Females and minorities in TV ads in 1987 Saturday children's programs. *Journalism Quarterly, 66,* 129–136.

Signorielli, N., McLeod, D., & Healy, E. (1994, Winter). Gender stereotypes in MTV commercials: The beat goes on. *Journal of Broadcasting and Electronic Media, 38,* 91–101.

Smith, L. J. (1994, Summer). A content analysis of gender differences in children's advertising. *Journal of Broadcasting and Electronic Media, 38,* 323–337.

Steele, J. R. (1999, November). Teenage sexuality and media practice: Factoring in the influences of family, friends, and school. *Journal of Sex Research, 36,* 4. Retrieved July 16, 2002, from EBSCOhost.

Steinke, J. (1998, Winter). Connecting theory and practice: Women scientist role models in television programming. *Journal of Broadcasting and Electronic Media, 42,* 142–151.

Subervi-Velez, F. A., & Colsant, S. (1993). The television worlds of Latino children. In G. L. Berry & J. K. Asamen (Eds.), *Children and television: Images in a changing sociocultural world* (pp. 215–242). Newbury Park, CA: Sage.

Tan, A., Fujioka, Y., & Lucht, N. (1997, Summer). Native American stereotypes, TV portrayals, and personal contact. *Journalism and Mass Communication Quarterly, 74,* 265–284.

Tapper, J., Thorson, E., & Black, D. (1994, Winter). Variations in music videos as a function of their musical genre. *Journal of Broadcasting and Electronic Media, 38,* 103–113.

Taylor, C. R., and Bang, H. (1997, Summer). Portrayals of Latinos in magazine advertising. *Journalism and Mass Communication Quarterly, 74,* 285–303.

Tucker, L. R. (1997, Winter). Was the revolution televised? Professional criticism about "The Cosby Show" and the essentialization of black cultural expression. *Journal of Broadcasting and Electronic Media, 41,* 90–108.

PART III

Empowering Audiences

Role of Parents and Families

Children develop their identities from many factors including mass media, but parents play a significant role in their children's relationship to mass media by their behavior as well as their words. The role of parents in the relationship of children to the media has run the gamut from all media, all day to no media, any day. A literary version of the all media, all day extreme can be seen in Dahl's (1988) *Matilda*, the story of a child prodigy whose parents prefer television to books. In the following excerpt, 5-year-old Matilda tries to get away from the TV:

> They were in the living-room eating their suppers on their knees in front of the telly. The suppers were TV dinners in floppy aluminum containers with separate compartments for the stewed meat, the boiled potatoes and the peas. Mrs. Wormwood sat munching her meal with her eyes glued to the American soap opera on the screen....
>
> "Mummy," Matilda said, "would you mind if I ate my supper in the dining-room so I could read my book?"
>
> The father glanced up sharply, "I would mind!" he snapped. "Supper is a family gathering and no one leaves the table till it's over!"
>
> "But we're not at the table," Matilda said. "We never are. We're always eating off our knees and watching the telly."
>
> "What's wrong with watching the telly, may I ask?" the father said. His voice had suddenly become soft and dangerous.
>
> Matilda didn't trust herself to answer him, so she kept quiet. (pp. 27–28)

In the film version, Matilda uses her powers of concentration to blow up the television in protest of her parents' behavior. The literary presentation is the opposite of what we might expect of the roles of parents and children regarding media.

Parents do determine how often children view or use media, but usually it is to restrict the number of hours they view. With television, for example, most researchers suggest children watch no more than an hour a day to avoid the problems of heavy viewing. The more children view media, cultivation analysis tells us, the more their perceptions of what is real are based on what they view. The importance of the program or media event to the child also plays a role in the impact the program will have. Family communication style and modeling have been shown to be important factors. Even physical arrangements such as whether youth have a TV or computer in their own rooms have been shown to be a significant variable. Competing activities are important with or without media.

Some researchers agree in a context reminiscent of Niebuhr's (1960) *Moral Man and Immoral Society* (see chapter 1). Niebuhr said that people are moral, but society is not. Society's values may be reflected in the media, but the theory states that only people and in the case of children's issues, parents, can make the moral judgments and teach morality. For some parents, that means eliminating television altogether. The other end of the spectrum from Matilda's family is the family that chooses no electronic media. Pipher (1996) presented anecdotes of families who have chosen the no media option.

> I encourage families to make conscious choices about media. I know a man who loves the ancient Greeks and who reads his children only books written before 1900. He allows no TV or radio in his home. His children love literature and are calmer and more relaxed than most children I know. Another family sold their TV and gave their children the money from its sale. The kids bought hiking boots and snowshoes and soon forgot that they ever had a TV. (p. 147)

Winn's (1985) book *Plug in Drug* suggests eliminating television. Most families are in between. They allow the TV and other media in their home, but with a range of rules and customs. Without supervision, children will use a lot more media than they will with parental supervision. The children who watch the most adult entertainment programming have parents who neither encourage nor regulate viewing (Wright, St. Peters, & Huston, 1990). These children are the ones most at risk.

The myth about parents' roles is that children watch too much violence due to parental neglect or absence. The reality is that the amount of television watched by children does not differ if parents are present or not. The truth is that parents do not restrict viewing for school-age children: "Survey studies of children in middle childhood and adolescence have demonstrated repeatedly that most parents do not regulate their children's television viewing" (Huston et al., 1992, p. 99). It's a case of children doing as their parents do.

> Parents play a crucial role in socializing viewing habits, largely through their own use of television. Parents also influence children's viewing by encouraging children to watch good programs and regulating what and how much television their children watch. When parents watch television with their children, they can use the

FIG. 7.1.   Families sometimes play a restrictive role in children's use of mass media. Kelty McGonagle, age 10, illustrates one way families may mediate children's viewing. Reprinted with permission.

opportunity to help children learn to counteract negative messages. However, evidence to date suggests that parents do not take full advantage of the opportunities afforded by coviewing. (p. 112)

To the extent that cultivation theory assumes that what you see is what you believe and that personal reality becomes the same as television reality, some of the researchers on family contexts disagree with cultivation theory. They advocate a child- or teen-centered look:

In general, the data support the theory of an active, selective child viewer, who applies rational, complex intrapersonal analysis strategies to media material, depending on the context, and whose parents affect this process through interpersonal communication about the material. They further point to family, as a real-life referent for comparison, as a reliable source of information about the media and the rest of the world, and as a fundamental aid, helping the child develop sophisticated strategies for analyzing the media world. (Austin & Roberts, 1990, p. 8)

In addition to looking at a child-centered, active viewer, recent research looks at the complexity of the cognitive processing of the media content (Thompson, Walsh-Childers, & Brown, 1993).

FAMILY COMMUNICATION PATTERNS

What a child or youth brings to the viewing experience in what they know cognitively and how they have developed their schemata sets the stage (Thompson et al., 1993). Family communication patterns also are part of the stage on which the media experiences take place. Two dimensions of family communication patterns are socio-orientation and concept orientation:

> Socio-orientation refers to family attitudes and norms toward social behavior and the extent to which parents encourage deference, social harmony, and pleasant relationships within the family. Socio-oriented homes may foster conformity and encourage children to give in on arguments rather than offending others or hurting their feelings. Concept orientation, on the other hand, is an information-focused communication norm related to attitudes toward objects and ideas. Concept-oriented parents emphasize the importance of considering and discussing all sides of an issue before making decisions. (Thompson et al., 1993, pp. 250–251)

In concept-oriented homes, adolescents apply media content in knowing more about and using more complex thinking about public affairs and in becoming more active and knowledgeable consumers. In socio-oriented homes, the adolescents apply media content to their own lives and use the behaviors as models (Thompson et al., 1993).

Parental Mediation

Just as children are active in the media use process, parents must also be active. Only if the parents are active can they be effective:

> There is evidence that parents can be effective if they choose to take an active role in mediation by structuring viewing rules and limits, providing brief and nondirective commentary while coviewing, being available for discussion to explain or expand on content, and helping children facilitate the internalization of critical viewing skills. (Soderman, Greenberg, & Linsangen, 1993, p. 164)

Mediation is the term commonly used to describe active discussion of media content (Austin, Bolls, Fujioka, & Engelbertson, 1999). Parents do not choose to mediate their children's use of mass media very often, but the use of three mediation tools can refute or reinforce media content:

Parental mediation involves three tasks: *categorization*, showing whether and how television reflects the real world; *validation*, involving endorsement or condemnation of portrayals; and *supplementation*, pointing out the usefulness of information from television by supplying additional information or by engaging in related activities. All three of these tasks can refute or reinforce television content by suggesting that television messages are/are not realistic, are right/wrong, and are/are not applicable to real-life situations. (Austin et al., 1999, p. 177)

Thus the parent or other person viewing with the child can also be critical to the viewing process.

Active, Restrictive, and Coviewing. Research in the last 20 years has identified three types of parental mediation as seen in three types of parental behavior: "talking to children about television or 'active mediation,' setting rules or restrictions regarding television viewing or 'restrictive mediation'; and watching television with children, or 'coviewing'" (Nathanson & Cantor, 2000, p. 125). (Note that Bybee, Robinson, & Turow [1982] claimed they were the first researchers to develop a multidimensional concept, calling the dimensions restrictive, evaluative, and unfocused.)

Nathanson (2001) conducted a survey of second- to sixth-grade children and their parents. To assess the type of mediation, children were asked the following questions: for active mediation—"When I watch TV shows with lots of fighting, my parents talk to me about them"; for restrictive mediation—"My parents have rules about how many TV shows with lots of fighting I can watch"; for coviewing—"When I watch TV shows with lots of fighting, my parents watch with me" (p. 209).

The three forms of mediation—active, restrictive, and coviewing—are distinct. Active mediation of television has the positive outcomes of encouraging skepticism toward news, creating a better understanding of narrative plots, and lowering aggression levels. Although restrictive mediation also has been linked with positive outcomes, it can be detrimental if the restrictiveness is too extensive. The outcomes for coviewing are mixed. On the positive side, children can get a better understanding of educational content. On the negative side, they may consider some characters real when they are not and they may become more aggressive.

The perception that violent television can be harmful predicted an action for both active mediation and restrictive mediation parents. In addition, for the restrictive mediation parents, it may be that their own dislike of violent media leads them to restrict this type of content for their children. On the other hand, those coviewing with children had a more positive attitude about violent content (Nathanson, 2001).

Which parents participate in these behaviors? Mothers, those with a more formal education, parents of younger children, parents concerned with the effects of aggression and fright, and heavy viewers have been identified as mediators of children's viewing. A Dutch study done by Valkenburg, Krcmar, Peeters, and Marseille (1999) found mothers were in the restrictive and instructive (another term used for active mediation) mode more frequently than fathers, perhaps because of their traditional position as primary caregivers. More formally educated parents also were found in the restrictive and instructive group. Parents of younger children were found there, but their concerns for negative effects seemed to be the real reason parents of younger children engaged in restrictive and instructive mediation more often (Valkenburg et al., 1999). Social coviewing occurred for those parents who viewed a lot of television. The authors concluded coviewing may be seen as a way of spending time together.

Coviewing is the least deliberate and least child-centered activity. It usually occurs when parent and child enjoy the same programming. In addition, coviewing has the potential of becoming active mediation: "Parents can be certain what children are watching, help them to understand the medium and its content, encourage them to accept only desirable or undesirable content, and gain firsthand knowledge of children's reactions to the medium and its content" (Dorr, Kovaric, & Doubleday, 1989, p 35). Dorr et al. (1989) found "that parents are more inclined to view with their children when they value television, value the particular type of content, and believe that children can learn from it" (p. 48).

However, coviewing alone is ineffective. Austin et al. (1999) "support ... the contention that coviewing and critical or analytical parental discussion of content are conceptually distinct.... Coviewing by parents appears unlikely without other influences to develop critical viewing skills in children" (p. 189).

The popular advice to coview with children may not provide any protection from the negative effects of television. In fact research shows that children may consider coviewing a parental endorsement for the behavior they see on television or in other media. Whereas active mediation and restrictive mediation may reduce antisocial effects through parental intervention, coviewing does not. Perhaps coviewing of violence and other antisocial content should be avoided to reduce the possibility that children will see it as a signal that the content is acceptable to the parent (Nathanson, 2001).

Media in the Home. Because children's media are home utilities, the number and location in the home are important factors in parents' mediation and family use. A 2000 survey of parents of children 2 to 17 years old and children 8 to 16 years old showed that almost half of the families had all four of the media being measured: television, VCR, video game equipment, and a computer. Many of these media are in children's bedrooms, where it is very difficult to exercise any parental mediation. It is interesting to note that the media were more likely to be found in the bedrooms of children from lower income families than from higher income families and largely in adolescent bedrooms (60%). Low-income families, however, had fewer computers and less Internet access.

The quantity of media use is more than 6 hours per day (Woodard & Gridina, 2000). The more sets, the less restrictive the style. The fewer the children, the more unfocused the guidance methods (van der Voort, Nikken, & van Lil, 1992). In an effort to determine how parents were using the government's policies of the 3-hour rule (CTA; see chapter 9) and V-chip, researchers used focus groups of children and mothers for Grades 3, 6, and 9. They found that as of the year 2000, parents did not use the new government policies in their mediation, but depended on their own experience and their children's preferences:

> Parents do not actively seek out external information about programming for chil-
> dren. Instead, they base their television-related rules on personal experiences, ad-
> vertisements, or the time that a program airs....

> Children make viewing decisions without their parents' help. They report turning
> to a specific channel that they like, looking for a specific show, flipping through pre-
> ferred channels until they find something that they like, or going to the Preview
> Channel....

> Multiple media compete for children's time and their interests in TV, the Internet,
> video games, and music changes constantly ... Parents' concerns about media ebb
> and flow based on their children's interest in the medium and their own level of
> comfort with it. (Schmitt, 2000, p. 3)

Considering media practices, there seems to be little awareness of the 3-hour rule or V-chip technology. Parents could not think of 3 hours of educational on commercial television.

Although government policy does not seem to have an effect on parental mediation, the findings do support the view that parents consider their mediation with children important and they talk to their children about television content and watch with them. However, what they coview is not educational television, but adult programs. Other findings include the trend that television rules for children become fewer as the child gets older (Schmitt, 2000).

Children seem to know more about age ratings than parents. Neither mothers nor children seem to be familiar with content ratings that can be used to tie into V-chip technology. Children know more about content ratings than mothers including what E / I (Educational / Informational) means and report watching educational shows, although ninth-grade boys do not think there are programs rated educational for their age. Third graders reported viewing animal and science educational programs; older children define educational as anything that gives them information about relationships (Schmitt, 2000).

In a related survey on media in the home, parents demonstrated a poor understanding about ratings, considering *Oprah* as educational television: "Many parents (71%) thought *Oprah* received a label designating it educational for children" (Woodard & Gridina, 2000, p. 4). However, more than half of the parents with the capability to block programming did engage it (V-chip). A much larger proportion (88%) of parents said they supervise television than said they supervise Internet or video games (about half).

MEDIATION INVOLVING SEXUALITY AND VIOLENCE

Besides asking what conditions are present for the various mediation styles, researchers also have asked what the effects are of television mediation (see Fig. 7.2). That research deals with the two effect areas of most concern dealt with in chapter 5, sexuality and violence.

FIG. 7.2.   Calvin questions why his dad's life is not like TV and suffers the consequences. CALVIN AND HOBBES © Watterson. Reprinted with permission of UNIVERSAL PRESS SYNDICATE. All rights reserved.

Sexuality and Mediation

On issues of sexuality, mediational variables have been found to be very prominent. Michigan study researchers concluded that if an adolescent engaged in media with sexual messages in the presence of friends or family, there was much more of these kinds of experiences for the teen:

> The largest set of variables was mediational: going out to movies with boy/girl-friends … and other friends …, seeing R-rated movies with a parent …, watching TV with other friends …, plus a lack of TV rules at home … were all positively linked to watching R-rated movies on videocassette recorders. (Greenberg et al., 1993, p. 94)

Mediation provided by the two original parents seems to predict the least exposure to sexual content:

> The presence of both original parents was associated with less television viewing overall, in prime-time and in the daytime, and with less exposure to television content containing portrayals of and references to sexual activities. This same correlate was predictive of a smaller diet of R-rated movies.

Another family variable—adolescents with nonworking mothers (mother at home)—was negatively related to exposure to television sexual content, and to watching R-rated movies on VCRs. In contrast, adolescents with a single parent—their mother—were more likely to spend more time watching TV at all times. (Greenberg et al., 1993, p. 86)

These findings can be interpreted in a couple of different ways: "At face value, the 'traditional' nuclear family appears to either afford or encourage fewer of these kinds of media experiences, or systematically provides more options" (Greenberg et al., 1993, p. 95).

Stanley and Greenberg (1993) summarized the same data as related to family structure and sexual messages:

Those with two original parents are best characterized, in terms of these media orientations and self-perceptions, by their smaller ratio of R-rated movies, by their nonattendance at R-rated movies with a parent, and by their greater use of the VCR for R-rated movies with lesser use for PG films. They are also most involved in school activities and exhibit the most satisfaction with their family situation. (p. 159)

Exposure to the sexual messages, however, is not the whole story. In addition to the parental mediation, peer group integration seems to play an important role in vaccinating teens against the unreal television images. Buerkel-Rothfuss (1993) provided evidence that the more time adolescents spent watching TV, the more time they spent with family and the less time they spent with peers. The opposite was true with music. The more time adolescents spent with music, the less time they spent with family. For some, this correlates with the theme of rock music as anti-establishment and anti-adult values (Buerkel-Rothfuss, 1993). On the other hand, the more integrated adolescents are in their peer group, the more immune they are to the distorted perceptions of reality found in some mass media images. In addition, the more discussion parents had with adolescent children about television, the less likely the teens were to have worldviews that reflected television reality.

Violence and Mediation

Media violence is another area in which parental mediation has been tested. In particular, active mediation has been found to make a difference in the effects of viewing violence:

Experiments have revealed that children who hear negative comments about the violent acts in the television programs they view (e.g., "It is bad to fight. It is better to help.") exhibit less aggressive behavior ..., have lower tolerance for aggression ..., and express attitudes that are less aggressive after viewing ... than do other youngsters. Because these studies were not part of lengthy media literacy programs, they demonstrate that even very small doses of active mediation can have an immediate effect. (Nathanson & Cantor, 2000, p. 126)

Fictional involvement is a mediational device that gives the children viewers tools to analyze the messages and thus immunize themselves from the potential effects of pervasive media violence:

> An individual is fictionally involved when he or she recognizes or is aware of the thoughts and feelings of fictional characters.... (F)ictional involvement is the same as perspective-taking (i.e., seeing the world from the perspective of another individual) except that the target is a fictional character appearing in a book, movie or television program. Theoretical explanations for media effects imply that this kind of approach may be useful in counteracting some of the features that make children more likely to experience adverse affects from televised violence. (Nathanson & Cantor, 2000, p. 127)

One of the problems with media violence depictions is that there are rarely negative consequences illustrated, especially for the victim. Yet, "research has shown that exposure to the negative consequences of violence reduces a viewer's tendency to imitate that violence" (Nathanson & Cantor, 2000, p. 127).

In an experiment to test the effects of fictional involvement, children from second to sixth grades viewed a 5-minute episode of *Woody Woodpecker* in which a tree medic interrupts Woody's nap. Woody tries various violent acts to drive the man away and gets back to his nap after he knocks the man unconscious (Nathanson & Cantor, 2000). There were three groups of children: those who experienced the fictional involvement mediation, those with no mediation, and a control group that saw no television. The fictional involvement group received instructions to think about the tree medic and how he is thinking when things happen to him. The children were then asked what they thought about the most while they had viewed. They also responded to specific questions about how they would act in hypothetical situations, their perceptions of how justified the violence they had viewed was, an evaluation of the perpetrator of the violence, an evaluation of the victim, and whether or not they thought the show was funny.

Nathanson and Cantor (2000) found that the fictional involvement and mediation had changed the way the children had viewed the characters and violence. Asking children to think about how the victim felt changed the way they evaluated the character and the way they perceived the violence itself, with children finding it less justified (Nathanson & Cantor, 2000). Of course, not all children reacted the same. Boys seemed more affected than girls by the mediation. "Fictional involvement manipulation was effective in preventing boys from experiencing an increase in post-viewing aggressive tendencies" (Nathanson & Cantor, 2000, p. 136). On the other hand, girls' aggressive scores did not change by condition.

The researchers concluded that even sixth-grade boys watching a classic cartoon need mediation because they are susceptible to aggressive tendencies after viewing violence. In addition, "getting children to think about how the victim feels is an effective strategy for reducing boys' post-viewing aggressive tendencies" (Nathanson & Cantor, 2000, p. 137). Furthermore, the fictional involvement tool does not require a parent to be present and can be used in any viewing by the child. One drawback is that children enjoy the violence less with this strategy. However, perhaps the lesson is that violence should not be fun (Nathanson & Cantor, 2000). We take another look at tools that help to analyze the message in chapter 8.

Another violence study looked at parental concerns for the child's responses to viewing violence as a variable. The conclusions of this study are counterintuitive to what we might expect and therefore critical for parents to understand. The research shows that parents who are less concerned about the effects of television violence have children who have a greater preference for violent programs. Those children with this preference are also more aggressive:

> This suggests that children who are more susceptible are on average the very ones whose parents are less concerned. Presumably, children most in need of parental guidance are the least likely to get any. This finding casts doubts upon projects aiming at having parents help their children acquire and use critical viewing skills. These projects may very well reach those parents that need them least. (van der Voort et al., 1992, p. 342)

It is critical for parents to understand that if a child seems less touched by violence, that may be a danger sign that the child is being more affected than the child whose fear is pulling him or her away from the influence of the message. Children who seem less touched by violence may be more desensitized and more susceptible to enacting the violence. On the other hand, children displaying fear may be less susceptible to becoming violent.

SUGGESTIONS FOR PARENTS

In *Selling Out America's Children*, Walsh (1994) provided a list of suggestions for parents that summarizes some of the findings on the role of parents.

1. Avoid using television as a babysitter.
2. Limit the use of TV.
3. Watch TV together.
4. Examine how you use television yourself.
5. Establish some clear ground rules.
6. Use the VCR to your advantage.

7. Do not give the television the most prominent location in the house.
8. Keep television sets out of kids' rooms.
9. Make sure you know what a movie or video is about and what it's rated before you give permission to view it.
10. Use the radio, records, or tapes when the television is not on.
11. Provide alternative activities that are enjoyable. (pp. 47–48)

Suggestions for other elements of society are provided in chapter. There are various aids for parents as they deal with their children and the media including Kidsnet.

Kidsnet Helps Parents, Teachers, Industry

Nick News is doing a special, but it will not appear in the *TV Guide* because it is too late to meet the publishing deadlines. The Kidsnet Web page can get the news out to parents immediately. Teachers and parents would like to know more about the miniseries *Joan of Arc*. Kidsnet provides a curriculum guide and chats with the star actress and the researcher for sets and costumes. CBS is doing a School Breaks special, and 1 hour dealt with health issues including AIDS. Kidsnet develops a curriculum guide for use with the program titled, "What If I'm Gay?"

No one was marrying education and media when Karen Jaffe, Kidsnet Executive Director, began her work in 1985. Kidsnet is one of the American Library Association's more than 700 great sites for kids and those who care about them. Kidsnet has a Media Guide that lists programs and their intended audience by age. The Media Guide listings give information for parents about content and tips for teachers about off-air taping guidelines and links to the show or network Web page. The Media Guide is the place where alerts are posted for late-breaking programming not listed in the *TV Guide,* such as *Nick News* specials.

According to the Web page introduction, "Kidsnet is the only national non-profit computerized clearinghouse and information center devoted to children's television, radio, audio, video and multimedia." Kidsnet is funded by memberships from industry, Jaffe said. Professionals and parents are Kidsnet users and they have access to research and information from media networks. Kidsnet gets income from grants, projects, and writing author newsletter columns for organizations that serve teachers, principals, and music educators. Ten years ago Kidsnet began developing curriculum materials of broadcasting and cable programming. The broadcast networks provide the revenue for study guides mailed free to educators.

Kidsnet provides extensive information referenced by curriculum and grade level. What Kidsnet provides "allows professional or parent to help make wise decisions and make decisions in a wise way," Jaffe said. "Empowered with information, the parent or professional can begin to make choices. For example, the preschool parent needs to understand the needs and concerns of the child and watch with the child if the child is young.

Kidsnet can be found at http://www.kidsnet.org with links to other helpful Web sites.

SUMMARY

Parents and families play a crucial role in the media habits of children and youth. Who they are and what they do with their children and media goes beyond their family to create an environment for the larger society. However, society also has a role in helping to support families as they take on the job of raising children.

FOR FURTHER CONSIDERATION

1. Write an essay explaining how your family fits into the various categories presented in this chapter.
2. Develop a model that represents all the ways family impacts children and the media.
3. What literary references can you describe that comment on the relationship of children and parents and media?

REFERENCES

Austin, E. W., Bolls, P., Fujioka, Y., & Engelbertson, J. (1999). How and why parents take on the tube. *Journal of Broadcasting and Electronic Media, 43*, 175–192.

Austin, E. W., & Roberts, D. F. (1990, August). Influences of family communication on children's television-interpretation processes. *Communication Research, 17*, Retrieved March 13, 2000, from EBSCOhost.

Buerkel-Rothfuss, N. L. (1993). Background: What prior research shows. In B. S. Greenberg, J. D. Brown, & N. Buerkel-Rothfuss (Eds.), *Media, sex and the adolescent* (pp. 5–18). Cresskill, NJ: Hampton.

Bybee, C., Robinson, D., & Turow, J. (1982). Determinants of parental guidance of children's television viewing for a special subgroup: Mass media scholars. *Journal of Broadcasting, 26*, 697–710.

Dahl, R. (1988). *Matilda*. New York: Puffin Books.

Dorr, A., Kovaric, P., & Doubleday, C. (1989, Winter). Parent–child coviewing in television. *Journal of Broadcasting and Electronic Media, 33*, 35–51.

Greenberg, B. S., Linsangan, R., Soderman, A., Heeter, C., Lin, C., Stanley, C., et al. (1993). Adolescents' exposure to television and movie sex. In B. S. Greenberg, J. D. Brown, & N. Buerkel-Rothfuss (Eds.), *Media, sex and the adolescent* (pp. 61–98). Cresskill, NJ: Hampton.

Huston, A. C., Donnerstein, E., Fairchild, H., Feshbach, N. D., Katz, P., Murray, J. P., et al. (1992). *Big world, small screen: The role of television in American society.* Lincoln: University of Nebraska Press.

Nathanson, A. I. (2001). Parent and child perspectives on the presence and meaning of parental television mediation. *Journal of Broadcasting and Electronic Media, 43,* 201–220.

Nathanson, A. I., & Cantor, J. (2000). Reducing the aggression-promoting effect of violent cartoons by increasing children's fictional involvement with the victim: A study of active mediation. *Journal of Broadcasting and Electronic Media, 44,* 125–142.

Niebuhr, R. (1960). *Moral man and immoral society: A study in ethics and politics.* New York: Scribner's.

Pipher, M. (1996). *Shelter of each other: Rebuilding our families.* New York: Ballantine.

Schmitt, K. L. (2000). *Public policy, family rules and children's media use in the home* (The Annenberg Public Policy Center of the University of Pennsylvania, Report Series No. 35). Executive summary retrieved July 8, 2000, from http://www.appcpenn.org/mediainhome/childrren/ppfr.pdf

Soderman, A., Greenberg, B. S., & Linsangan, R. (1993). Pregnant and non-pregnant adolescents' television and movie experiences. In B. S. Greenberg, J. D. Brown, & N. Buerkel-Rothfuss (Eds.), *Media, sex and the adolescent* (pp. 163–173). Cresskill, NJ: Hampton.

Stanley, C., & Greenberg, B. S. (1993). Family structure and adolescents' orientation to TV and movie sex. In B. S. Greenberg, J. D. Brown, & N. Buerkel-Rothfuss (Eds.), *Media, sex and the adolescent* (pp. 153–162). Cresskill, NJ: Hampton.

Thompson, M., Walsh-Childers, K., & Brown, J. D. (1993). The influence of family communication patterns and sexual experience on processing of a music video. In B. S. Greenberg, J. D. Brown, & N. Buerkel-Rothfuss (Eds.), *Media, sex and the adolescent* (pp. 248–262). Cresskill, NJ: Hampton.

Valkenburg, P. M., Krcmar, M., Peeters, A. L., & Marseille, N. M. (1999, Winter). Developing a scale to assess three styles of television mediation: "Instructive mediation," "restrictive mediation," and "social coviewing." *Journal of Broadcasting and Electronic Media, 43,* 52–66.

Van der Voort, T. H. A., Nikken, P., & van Lil, J. E. (1992, Winter). Determinants of parental guidance of children's television viewing: A Dutch replication study. *Journal of Broadcasting and Electronic Media, 36,* 61–74.

Walsh, D. (1994). *Selling out America's children.* Minneapolis, MN: Deaconess.

Winn, M. (1985). *The plug-in drug: Television, children and the family* (rev. ed.). New York: Penguin.

Woodard, E. H., & Gridina, N. (2000). *Media in the home, 2000: The fifth annual survey of parents and children* (The Annenberg Public Policy Center of the University of Pennsylvania, Survey Series No. 7). Executive summary retrieved July 8, 2002, from http://www.appcpenn.org/mediainhome/survey/survey7.pdf

Wright, J. C., St. Peters, M., & Huston, A. (1990). Family television use and its relation to children's cognitive skills and social behavior. In J. Bryant (Ed.), *Television and the American family* (pp. 227–251). Hillsdale, NJ: Lawrence Erlbaum Associates.

Media Literacy and Positive Effects

THE DIARY OF A YOUNG GIRL

Saturday, June 20, 1942

Writing in a diary is a really strange experience for someone like me. Not only because I've never written anything before, but also because it seems to me that later on neither I nor anyone else will be interested in the musings of a thirteen-year-old schoolgirl. Oh well, it doesn't matter. I feel like writing, and I have an even greater need to get all kinds of things off my chest. (Frank, 1991, p. 6).

Friday, October 9, 1942

Dearest Kitty,

Today I have nothing but dismal and depressing news to report. Our many Jewish friends and acquaintances are being taken away in droves. The Gestapo is treating them very roughly and transporting them in cattle cars to Westerbrook, the big camp in Drenthe to which they're sending all the Jews.... The English radio says they're being gassed. (Frank, 1991, p. 54)

Tuesday, June 6, 1944

My dearest Kitty,

"This is D Day," The BBC announced at twelve. "This is *the* day." The invasion has begun! (Frank, 1991, p. 310)

Anne Frank did not survive the Holocaust. Although she lived to see D-Day, she and her family were arrested from their hiding place and she died of typhus at Bergen-Belsen shortly before British troops liberated the camp in 1945. Her diary lives today as an account of the trials of Jews in hiding during World War II. As with Anne Frank, the writing aspect of literacy includes the elements of self-clarification, individual empowerment, and even political repercussions.

119

MEDIA LITERACY: READING AND WRITING TEXTS

Like Anne Frank's use of her diary, media literacy today includes the use of electronic as well as print media to give voice to youth and to receive information. Various perceptions of power relationships have meant that media literacy has a wide range of definitions, types, and strategies. Hobbs (1998) gave perhaps the most inclusive definition:

> Media literacy has been defined as the ability to access, analyze, evaluate, and communicate messages in a wide variety of forms.... It is a term used by a growing number of scholars and educators to refer to the process of critically analyzing and learning to create one's own messages in print, audio, video, and multimedia. Its emphasis is on learning and teaching of these skills through using mass media texts in primarily school-based contexts. (p. 16)

Although Anne Frank did not exercise her media literacy in school or electronic media for obvious reasons, she was able to access information via BBC radio broadcasts and even newspapers in her hiding place. She analyzed what she heard based on her ability to read and listen critically. She evaluated based on her perception of the reliability of the source and her own experience. Finally she communicated, at first to her diary, Kitty, and ultimately to the world.

Media literacy today also includes these elements of identity, empowerment and politics. Like other theories we have considered, media literacy predicts types of behavior. Like our consideration of diverse identities, media literacy looks at how children and youth use the media to develop a self-identity. Like the chapter on the role of parents, this chapter looks at how parents and other adults may work with children and youth to develop media literacy to empower them both in use of media and in their work in the world.

Reading and writing seem to define print literacy, but even that definition has been argued. Reading at what level? What content? Print literacy was used as a political tool to deny people their right to vote during the pre-Civil Rights period in the South. When a very well-educated African American went to register to vote, he was given a literacy test that was geared to a very high level. "What does this mean?" asked the voter registrar. "It means you don't want me to vote," replied the man. Literacy is linked to politics because it is about power. If a citizen understands the communication of the powerful, it is possible to change the power arrangement, particularly if the individual can use the tools of communication. The First Amendment of the U.S. Constitution is based on the premise that if all people in a democratic republic have a voice, then the best ideas will be affirmed and the worst ideas will be lost. There is no democracy without the freedom of speech and freedom of the press.

For children, literacy in the media age is even more complex. The texts have multiplied and at the same time become more accessible to younger children. The texts on radio, television, and the Internet do not require learning to read. However, being able to watch television at a young age does not mean children understand it the same way adults do. Meyrowitz (1998) said that television is not a literacy subject in a traditional sense because children can watch it and understand without any instruction. Television is not like reading. The things that separate children from adults when it comes to television differ: "There is little, except an intervening adult, programmed V-chip, or sleep schedule, that demands that a young child watch *Mr. Rogers Neighborhood* before watching *NYPD Blue*" (Meyrowitz 1998, p. 107).

However, reading a text readily accessible even to small children is only half the task of literacy. The other half is writing. Lewis and Jhally (1998) compare television audiences to those in the early industrial revolution who were taught to read but not to write: "They are expected to consume rather than produce— to pick from the display offered by commercial television rather than debate the terms and conditions in which broadcasting takes place" (p. 111). Thus, in addition to being able to view the content critically, the concept of media literacy contains elements of being able to use the media, just as we learn to write.

PROSOCIAL MESSAGES, WORLDVIEW, AND STRATEGIES

Media literacy presumes that media are an acceptable part of the environment and have prosocial as well as antisocial messages. Mares (1996) summarized the prosocial research and positive effects: "Children exposed to prosocial content have more positive social interactions, show more altruistic behavior and self-control, and have less stereotyped views of others" (p. 19). In addition, prosocial content becomes stronger when discussion accompanies the message. Younger children and girls have the strongest effects from prosocial content.

Like Gerbner's cultivation theory, media literacy advocates do believe that children's programming presents a worldview. Silverblatt (1995) gave five aspects of the "distinct world view" he observed:

A homogenous world ...
A world filled with stereotypes ...
A violent world ...
An absolute world ...
A world run by children ... (p. 282)

By a homogenous world, Silverblatt (1995) meant there is little racial and ethnic diversity, but many stereotypes, including the gender stereotypes with boys as the active participants and girls as the passive observers or girls completely absent. The world of television is even more violent for children than adults, with Saturday morning cartoons displaying three times the violence of prime-time television. Children's television is absolute in that the characters are either good guys or bad guys and the programs offer simple solutions to difficult problems. Finally, the children's shows depict adults "as ignorant, close minded, or inept" (Silverblatt, 1995, p. 282). Therefore, "Kids are best served (in children's television) by bonding together in peer groups and keeping information from their parents" (p. 282).

FIG. 8.1.   Families can promote media literacy that helps inoculate children from negative effects as Jackie Todd, age 10, illustrates with her drawing of a family watching TV together. Reprinted with permission.

Silverblatt (1995) provided seven media literacy strategies for adults to use with children. The strategies emphasize the positive effects conditions including moderation, discussion, and active participation:

1. Moderation.
2. Participation with the child.
3. Discussion of the TV industry.
4. Discussion of the reality or fantasy of entertainment programming.
5. Talking back to your TV.
6. Presenting an understanding of TV.
7. Actively selecting programming. (Silverblatt, 1995, pp. 285–287)

Whereas moderation and participation with the child reflect a protectionist stance, discussion questions and active selection of programming reflect more of an acquisition of skills model (see below). Questions to ask children regarding the viewing experience include asking about explicit content, by asking, "What happened?" to provide "an opportunity for adults to clarify any misconceptions, fill in gaps, and learn about the child's interests and concerns" (Silverblatt, 1995, p. 287). Regarding affective or emotional response, two questions can be asked: "How did you feel during particular points of the story? How did you feel about certain aspects of the program? For instance, 'Did you like (a particular character)?' Why?" (p. 287)

For implicit content, ask why, especially regarding motives, such as "Why do you think he behaved like that?" (Silverblatt, 1995, p. 287). Other "why" questions have to do with function, such as asking why an ad was produced. Another topic with related questions is logical conclusion. Questions include: "Did you like the ending? Why or why not? If not, how *should* the program have ended? Why? How would you have *preferred* for the program to end? Why?" (p. 287). Finally, Silverblatt suggested questions about the intended audience because much of the programming children watch is designed for adults or older children.

More specific questions can be asked for certain age groups and situations. For example, Finders (1996) looked at seventh-grade girls and how they use teen magazines to rebel and become leaders of their peer groups by adopting the style and consumer values of the magazines. The media literacy she described is in the area of political and social roles. Finders (1996) suggested the following questions for adults and teachers to ask girls about teen magazines:

Who is being privileged? Why are these stories being told at this particular historic moment? How might the woman's role be represented differently at a different historic period? Whose interests are being served? Teaching early adolescents to ask questions about the sociocultural construction of roles will lead students to a deeper understanding of how textual representations reflect and define the roles available in the larger culture. (p. 86)

These types of questions go past information to the politics of the scripts girls may be learning from these sources.

AGREEMENT ON KEY CONCEPTS IN MEDIA LITERACY

To find agreement on media literacy concepts, Aufderheide (1997) presented a report of the National Leadership conference on Media Literacy: "A media literate person ... can decode, evaluate, analyze, and produce both print and electronic media" (p. 79). The three elements that come together to produce that media reality are the production process, the text (or message), and the audience. The production process in turn has elements that mold and constrain it including technology, economics, bureaucracy, and the law. Media educators agree on the following precepts:

- Media are constructed, and construct reality.
- Media have commercial implications.
- Media have ideological and political implications.
- Form and content are related in each medium, each of which has a unique aesthetic, codes, and conventions.
- Receivers negotiate meaning in media. (Aufderheide, 1997, p. 80)

Media are constructed; they are not reality but messages people put together. In turn they help to put together the reality the audience perceives. The media are commercial; they are paid for with advertising. The advertisers buy not space or air-time but a particular audience. The media do have their own ideological and political viewpoints, which may or may not be the same as that of the audience. Each medium is unique and needs to be understood as such. Receivers or the audience decide what the media messages mean, each from his or her own perspective.

DISAGREEMENTS IN THE MEDIA LITERACY DEBATES

For those who find media an acceptable part of the environment, various views or debates on media literacy differentiate the proponents. Hobbs (1998) presented seven questions we can see in the debate over media literacy today.

1. "Should Media Literacy Education Aim to Protect Children and Young People From Negative Media Influences?" (p. 18)

If the answer to the question is yes, Hobbs (1998) called it a protectionist stance that is teacher centered. If the answer is no, then the media literacy model is one of acquisition of skills to maximize positive effects (Desmond, 1997). The implication of early media education (before 1960) was that media education was educating young people against the media because the media are commercial and unproven low culture compared with the high culture of the classics, proven as to their value over time (Masterman, 1997). After 1960, the media education rationale was to educate young people to tell the difference between good and bad media.

The protectionist stand also focuses on the content of the media and fits into Meyrowitz's (1998) model of media content literacy. This model sees media as conduits that differ by form, but what is important is the content. Media literacy in this model is geared toward analyzing content. This model seems to contend that we then contrast one content element such as violence with another content element such as peacefulness.

Yet another way to characterize the protectionist view is with the analogy of inoculation. If someone is inoculated with a little bit of a dangerous germ, he or she can build up antibodies to fight off that germ. In the case of media literacy, viewing media with instruction, analysis, and evaluation can inoculate children and others against the harm that media might do (Brown, 1991; Davies, 1997; see alcohol research presented later).

Although there may be advantages to protecting children, the danger of a protectionist stance is that the teacher may present standard answers to be parroted back instead of a more authentic response from students (Hobbs, 1998).

2. "Should Media Production Be an Essential Feature of Media Literacy Education?" (Hobbs 1998, p. 20)

If the answer to the question is yes, then we have an acquisitions model that is maximizing positive effects. Developing those skills may require the experience of creating media including photography, videography, and Web page development (Hobbs, 1998).

Meyrowitz (1998) called the focus on production media grammar literacy, which focuses on each medium's production values and language. Media literacy in this model is geared to how each medium works and how each medium's grammar can be analyzed. In this case the content is constant and not the focus. In comparing the grammar variables, an example would be comparing a murder from two perspectives: that of the victim and that of the murderer.

Messaris (1998) gave the example of production grammar as seen in visual convention such as avoiding fades and dissolves in modern film and advertising work:

> Instead, filmmakers have come increasingly to rely on the viewer's ability to intuit the relationship between scenes on the basis of contextual cues.... As advertisers themselves have occasionally acknowledged, the lack of explicitness of visual syntax has a very important consequence for practitioners of visual persuasion: It makes it possible for them to convey persuasive messages in visual form that would be controversial or unacceptable if spelled out verbally. (p. 76)

For example, cigarette advertising often juxtaposes smokers with pristine natural landscapes and outdoor sports, perhaps to make cigarettes seem healthy. To say in words that smoking is healthy would be unacceptable today. However, to juxtapose a mountain lake or a healthy outdoor lifestyle with smoking can communicate the same message (Messaris, 1998).

For children, the television elements seem real. One way that children can get beyond the appearance of reality is by what Masterman (1997) called denaturalizing the media through revealing techniques, including discussion about how production occurs and techniques used to create the sense of reality. In addition, the media tend to normalize behaviors by repeating them and making ideas seem like common sense. How the audience responds to these efforts also can be discussed.

However, Lewis and Jhally (1998) said that there is no proof that students' ability to produce video translates into any type of analytical perspective. Furthermore, because of the cost of the equipment, it is a rich school system's option. Media production is both expensive and associated with more technical and therefore sometimes more vocational education. Both of these qualities make it difficult to support in poorly funded school systems and those in which the uses of media production are at odds with the more canon-oriented teaching of the classics of literature to the exclusion of popular culture.

The importance of production can be seen in the early response to cable television and the insistence on opportunities to gain production experience and access for citizens via public access channels. The tie between being able to use the production tools to add your voice to the medium and being empowered within the culture has been part of the theory behind public access channels on cable television. Today we see teens empowered with Web pages.

20 Below:
Newspapers Provide a Web Site for Teens

For Maine teenagers, newspapers online offer more than current events. Not only can teens write movie and music reviews, but they can review computer games as well. Writers can publish their views, stories, and poetry on the Web page. A University of Maine expert on family relations and human sexuality responds to specific questions from individual teens. Links back to Mainetoday.com provide a calendar and horoscope options, and school newspapers can contribute their materials to be published online.

The Web site was originally named Teen Go, but has changed its name to 20 Below and has won a national award. The Digital Edge Award (the Edgies), presented by the Newspaper Association of America's (NAA) New Media Federation, has recognized 20 Below (20below.mainetoday.com) for public service by a newspaper with circulation of less than 75,000.

The community coordinator for the *Portland Press Herald,* Jessica Tomlinson, and Web content provider and host Melissa Kim Phillips staff the Web site. In June 1998, the *Press Herald Online* started Teen Go as a place for Maine teens to publish their writing and opinions. Tomlinson observed that Portland teens were being marginalized in November 1998, before Columbine. Acting on her observations, Tomlinson won a grant from the Pew Center for Civic Journalism to support a project called Teen Voices that would look at issues currently facing teenagers on the Web site. Tomlinson joined with Phillips and kicked off the teen involvement with 60 disposable cameras given to teens in September 1999 at a pizza party. The teens used the disposable cameras to document their lives while stories were written by reporter Barbara Walsh. The series began in January 2000, first in the Sunday *Portland Press Herald* and also on the Teen Go / 20 Below Web site.

20 Below also provides story ideas for the education reporter at the *Portland Press Herald.* After listening to teens talk at the forum at which the cameras

were distributed, the education reporter picked up a story idea. "For instance, a teenager was talking about how she had hired a consultant to do her college applications," so Tomlinson said he did a story on that. Story ideas also develop from the chat room for the Web site. "There was a researcher from England who is doing her dissertation on Tommy's Park, which is this very popular park where teenagers hang out (in Portland), and it causes an interesting tension between city officials and teens about how that operates," Tomlinson said. The education reporter also did that story.

20 Below has an advice expert who is just for the Web page and is only found online. Advice expert Dr. Sandra Caron teaches courses in Family Relations and Human Sexuality at the University of Maine at Orono. The advice replies are a priority for Phillips. "Monday I got an advice letter," Phillips said and she quoted the letter: "'I really like this guy. We've been dating for two months. He says he'll call me but he doesn't.'... So I sent it to Sandy Caron," Phillips said. "She replied and then I sent a reply back to the kid as well as put it on the Web site, too. Cause I figured she's not going to want to wait a week to get an answer. So I did that right away and put it on the site as well."

3. "Should Media Literacy Focus on Popular Culture Texts?" (Hobbs, 1998, p. 21)

The key to the answer to this question is whether or not the ability to analyze popular culture texts can be transferred to other types of text analysis. If it is transferable, then media literacy could focus on popular culture texts and teachers would be confident students could use those same skills to analyze other texts, achieving an important pedagogical goal. Hobbs (1998) explained that focusing on popular culture is what makes media literacy different from other types of literacy, such as information literacy or computer literacy. Under the acquisition model, skills developed from the use of popular media as the first text can then be transferred to other texts, "how lessons from home entertainment and in school viewing are or could be applied to other domains of learning" (Desmond, 1997, pp. 338–339). Whether the concerns are transfer of skills from popular culture to classical culture or transfer of understanding from school to home, such transfers form the basis of some disagreements among media literacy researchers and require further study.

4. "Should Media Literacy Have a More Explicit Political and Ideological Agenda?" (Hobbs, 1998, p. 22)

This question provides a big point of departure for those who believe that all messages have a political or social message and therefore should be analyzed with politics and ideological repercussions in mind. Whether from the left or right, many who advocate for media literacy have a political or social agenda they are using to determine whether a message is acceptable or not. According to Hobbs (1998), most teachers will try to give the student the tools to analyze without any particular agenda in mind. Rather, most teachers try to promote each student's ability to critically analyze media information. By doing so, the teacher aims to

> maximize the students' potential for discovery and the realization of personal, social, or political action without pushing a specific agenda on students.... There is an obvious ideology that underlies even the most basic tenets of media literacy education—teaching students to question textual authority and to use reasoning to reach autonomous decisions. (Hobbs, 1998, p. 23)

The questioning of authority and the individual decision making is, according to its advocates, a radical stance that goes as far as necessary to empower students.

McLuhan and others offered the concept that regardless of content or production grammar, each medium creates an environment that differs in how both content and production values are organized (see chapter 1). Meyrowitz (1998) called this medium literacy because you focus on the environment of the individual medium:

> On the micro, single-situation level, medium analyses look at the implications of choosing one medium versus another for a particular communication. Macro, societal-level medium analyses explore how the widespread use of a new medium leads to broad social changes. (p. 105)

In medium literacy the focus goes beyond grammar to how the medium is used. For example, e-mail could be compared to a telephone call. If we examine when an individual would choose the telephone and when the individual would choose e-mail, we are looking at the microlevel. If we examine how the choices of each medium may affect interpersonal relations, we are looking at the macrolevel. Different skills are required to use various media, such that literacy is not the same in each medium. There are political implications for what Meyrowitz (1998) called medium literacy today for educators because "the many relatively new, non-reading ways to gain access to information now weaken the informational power of the school and diminish the incentives to learn to read and write well" (p. 107). Thus the schools are being challenged, as well as the parents in the transition from a print-based culture to a multimedia-based culture.

Others, however, believe that the political and social analysis needs to be more overt and obvious to the students:

> To evaluate those messages, students must learn to see them not simply as true or false, realistic or misleading, stereotypical or positive, but as authored voices with

certain interests or assumptions about the world, voices that could be influenced or replaced.... It is important to note that we are not advocating propagandizing in schools for a particular political perspective. We are advocating a view that recognizes that the world is always made by someone, and a decision to tolerate the status quo is as political as a more overtly radical act. (Lewis & Jhally, 1998, p. 119)

Concerns about overt or covert power relationships will not be resolved, but these concerns need to be on the table in the continuing discussions of media literacy education.

5. "Should Media Literacy Be Focused on School-Based K–12 Educational Environments?" (Hobbs, 1998, p. 23)

Outside the United States (e.g., Europe, Australia, and Canada), there are more school-based literacy projects. However, there are some problems attaining these projects in the United States. "The United States finds itself in the ironic position of being the world's leading exporter of media products while lagging behind every other major English-speaking country in the world in the formal delivery of media education in its schools" (Kubey, 1998, p. 58). In foreign countries that are deluged with American media, people react from fear of being overwhelmed by American culture: "In short, there is a hope in many countries ... that media education will help their youth perceive that the values promulgated in the U.S. and other countries' media products are not necessarily their own" (Kubey, 1998, p. 63). The United States does not have that impetus of the threat of foreign media because there are few foreign media in the United States.

Other cultural issues that also work against media education include our diversity, our attitude toward teachers, and the crowded curriculum. Our diversity makes it more difficult for us to agree on things. In particular, Kubey (1998) said, because of our diversity, it is more difficult for parents to see educational authorities as sharing their values. In addition, U.S. teachers are not respected for their knowledge the way teachers are respected in other countries. One more thing in a crowded curriculum is also difficult to manage. Due to other priorities for time and commitment to the canon, it is tough to get media literacy into the schools; however, after-school programs are seen as an accessible option (Hobbs, 1998).

6. "Should Media Literacy Be Taught as a Specialist Subject or Integrated Within the Context of Existing Subjects?" (Hobbs, 1998, p. 25)

Most media educators agree that teaching media literacy across the curriculum is the best option: "Media literacy modules can be integrated efficiently within existing courses and curricula. Although not ideal, this option meets less resistance to scheduling and competent staffing" (Brown, 1991, p. 52). However, media literacy across the curriculum also can marginalize the media literacy and make it invisible. "This approach carries with it the potential for students to gain exposure to media analysis and production activities, even though it risks trivializing analysis and production if underqualified teachers engage in the work" (Hobbs, 1998, p. 25).

7. "Should Media Literacy Initiatives Be Supported Financially by Media Organizations?" (Hobbs, 1998, p. 26)

Media organizations from newspapers to cable companies have provided materials for media literacy. Some see this as their responsibility. However, that provision also can be seen as muting the criticism of the media organizations providing the information. Always ask who is sponsoring the message and why.

In sum, Hobbs (1998) advocated a "pedagogy of inquiry" (p. 27). Media literacy education is "asking questions about media texts" (p. 27). Such an open-ended approach also can help to ensure the survival of media literacy education, perhaps because there is no political agenda and the approach fits with the teaching style teachers can easily use in the classroom.

MEDIA LITERACY AND RESEARCH

The American Academy of Pediatrics (1999) summarized some of the research on the effectiveness of media education:

> Research strongly suggests that media education may result in young people becoming less vulnerable to negative aspects of media exposure. In several studies, children in elementary school-based programs were able to evaluate program and advertising content more critically. In other studies, heavy viewers of violent programming were less accepting of violence or showed decreased aggressive behavior after a media education intervention. A recent study found a change in attitudes regarding intention to drink alcohol after a media education program. (p. 2)

The studies take an inoculation approach that says that the skills being taught in the program protect the child from negative effects. One study on alcohol compared a general media literacy program to one specifically geared to alcohol advertising comparing third-grade boys and girls. The premise of the study was that early inoculation of media literacy programs for third graders would help protect those children from alcohol abuse. The study found even a general media literacy training program "can reduce expectancies and the propensity toward an unhealthy behavior" (Austin & Johnson, 1997, p. 35), but lessons on alcohol advertising portrayals "are likely to have a stronger and longer lasting effect" (p. 37). As might be expected, boys and girls differ in their response to alcohol advertising. For example, "boys had more positive expectancies and showed a stronger preference for beer-related products than girls" (p. 37). Austin and Johnson (1997) suggested designing different decision-making interventions for boys and girls: "For boys, for example, priority may be given to finding ways to establish supportive relationships while nevertheless appearing strong and in no need of support. For girls, priority may be given to appearing attractive and popular, rather than strong" (p. 37).

In addition to different decision-making interventions, boys and girls seem to respond differently to broad versus focused messages. Boys needed the media literacy lesson that was specific to alcohol consumption, whereas girls could get the same benefit from a more general media literacy program:

> The alcohol-specific treatment condition seemed more important for boys, whereas girls were affected by both general and alcohol-specific media literacy training. This finding may suggest that girls generalize the lessons better to specific contexts not covered in the training, or it may suggest that boys need stronger defenses against advertising targeting them more specifically. (Austin & Johnson, 1997, p. 39)

Media literacy programs are usually geared to middle school or older elementary-age students, but Austin and Johnson (1997) showed that younger children do benefit from this earlier intervention: "Schools ... may find general media literacy training a promising avenue for providing children with an early health promotion and substance abuse prevention message, without risking the communitywide controversy that an alcohol-specific program geared to young children might inspire" (p. 39).

One of the problems of introducing media literacy programs in schools is the need for financing the programs. Early intervention with media literacy programs can be effective in curbing anticipated alcohol abuse and these programs are deserving of such funding. In particular, items used in the promotion of alcohol such as toy trucks with beer ads on them should be restricted.

> When beer and tobacco brands and mascots are as familiar to young children as Mickey Mouse, and children are finding them desirable as well, it should cause public concern.... (S)ome action seems warranted to provide special protection to children younger than 10 from marketing efforts they are unprepared to resist. (Austin & Johnson, 1997, p. 40)

Austin and Johnson (1997) concluded that early media literacy benefits children much as an inoculation from disease by providing decision-making skills related to responses to media messages: "Once children master a decision-making skill, they apply it to a variety of contexts.... For long-term benefits, then, it seems more valuable to concentrate on helping children develop skills for making decisions than to teach them which specific decisions to make" (p. 40).

Other research indicates that in addition to promoting good decision making, media experiences in combination with instruction can prepare children for dangers. Cantor and Omdahl (1999) found that for children who both viewed a dramatized media depiction of an accident and received safety guidelines afterward, the children perceived the guidelines as high in importance. When children are afraid or find out about a danger, they try to lessen the fear or fight the danger. Even those viewing only the dramatized accident without any instruction saw the importance of safety more than those who had not. Live television news may provide opportunities.

> When the mass media thrust such incidents on our children, we may want to use such incidents as "teachable moments" and make the best of a bad situation. Alternatively, adults seeking effective times and methods for teaching safety guidelines may want to present dramatizations of realistic threats that children will probably be exposed to anyway. (Cantor & Omdahl, 1999, p. 69)

Cultivation theory predicts that children will feel more vulnerable rather than raising their awareness of specific threats. There are a variety of online resources, for example, to enable adults to help children to turn their fears, such as prompted by the events of September 11, 2001, into constructive action.

SUMMARY

From Anne Frank's diary to children's Web pages, the voices of youth are important for them to express and adults to hear. Media literacy education expands our view of literacy from print to screens of television and Internet communication. Media literacy can be seen as protection of children through inoculation or education to wisely acquire and use effectively a variety of skills specific to a variety of media. The skills range from understanding and analyzing a message to evaluating and giving feedback using the appropriate production skills. Research is establishing the importance of media literacy education at an early age to foster both general decision-making skills and specific analysis of messages such as those that may promote alcohol or cigarettes.

FOR FURTHER CONSIDERATION

1. Austin and Johnson (1997) suggested a *Magic School Bus* type of program for media. Develop your own program description and episode of The Magic Cyber Bus that would take children on rides through the world of radio, broadcast television, cable television, VCR, or the Internet, explaining formal features and other elements of media literacy.

2. It is interesting to note that the Austin and Johnson (1997) research reported earlier was supported in part by the Alcoholic Beverage Medical Research Foundation. Find out who they are and establish what (if any) bias that might have introduced to the research reported by Austin and Johnson.

3. Choose a subject and compare various media presentations of the subject such as the Holocaust, the Civil War or any other topic (Bianculli, 1992, p. 186).

4. Choose a movie to analyze in terms of the use of production grammar from a child's point of view. For example, the use of transitions in the movie *The Sixth Sense* fool the viewer into believing that the child psychologist, who has been shot by one of his patients, is alive. The intention is to mislead the audience because the character himself does not realize he is dead, but children might not understand that, in fact, he was dead even at the end of the movie. The transitions did not provide that understanding. They were purposefully vague. A child also might think the little boy who could see dead people was the same boy who had shot the child psychologist.

5. Choose one of Silverblatt's (1995) worldview statements or one of these: Might makes right, or the end justifies the means. Identify specific media messages you believe send this message to children.

6. Loewen (1995) wrote a book called *Lies My Teacher Told Me*. Generate a list of lies you believe the mass media tell children. Give specific examples in an essay on "Lies the Mass Media Tell Children."

RESOURCES ON THE WEB

- 20 Below Web site for Maine teens: http://www.20below.mainetoday.com/
- The re: constructions project at http://web.mit.edu/cms/reconstructions/ deals with the media's role during the September 11 crisis.
- Friendship Through Education at http://www.FriendshipThroughEducation.org/ creates links between U.S. students and Muslim students abroad.
- Culture Goggles at http://www.nationalgeographic.com/xpenditions/hall?node=27/ is the National Geographic site that shows how Jerusalem is viewed by Judaism, Islam, and Christianity.

REFERENCES

American Academy of Pediatrics, Committee on Public Education. (1999, August). Media education (RE 9911). *Pediatrics, 104*, 341–343. Retrieved 2000 from http://www.aap.org/policy/re9911.html

Aufderheide, P. (1997). Media literacy: From a report of the National Leadership Conference on Media Literacy. In R. Kubey (Ed.), *Media literacy in the information age: Current perspectives, information and behavior* (Vol. 6, pp. 79–86). New Brunswick, NJ: Transaction.

Austin, E. W., & Johnson, K. K. (1997). Effects of general and alcohol-specific media literacy training on children's decision making about alcohol. *Journal of Health Communication, 2*, 17–42.

Bianculli, D. (1992). *Teleliteracy: Taking television seriously.* New York: Continuum.

Brown, J. A. (1991). *Television "critical viewing skills" education: Major media literacy projects in the United States and selected countries.* Hillsdale, NJ: Lawrence Erlbaum Associates.

Cantor, J., & Omdahl, B. L. (1999). Children's acceptance of safety guidelines after exposure to televised dramas depicting accidents [Electronic version]. *Western Journal of Communication, 63,* 57–71.

Davies, M. M. (1997). *Fake, fact, and fantasy: Children's interpretation of television reality.* Mahwah, NJ: Lawrence Erlbaum Associates.

Desmond, R. (1997). Media literacy in the home: Acquisition versus deficit models. In R. Kubey (Ed.), *Media literacy in the information age: Current perspectives, information and behavior* (Vol. 6, pp. 323–343). New Brunswick, NJ: Transaction.

Finders, M. J. (1996). Queens and teen zines: Early adolescent females reading their way toward adulthood. *Anthropology and Education Quarterly, 27,* 71–89.

Frank, A. (1991). *The diary of a young girl: The definitive edition.* New York: Anchor Books.

Hobbs, R. (1998). The seven great debates in the media literacy movement. *Journal of Communication, 48,* 16–32.

Kubey, R. (1998). Obstacles to the development of media education in the United States. *Journal of Communication, 48,* 58–69.

Lewis, J., & Jhally, S. (1998). The struggle over media literacy. *Journal of Communication, 48,* 109–120.

Loewen, J. (1995). *Lies my teacher told me: Everything your American history textbook got wrong.* New York: Simon & Schuster.

Mares, M. (1996). *Positive effects of television on social behavior: A meta-analysis.* Philadelphia: Annenberg Public Policy Center of the University of Pennsylvania. Retrieved July 2002 from www.appcpenn.org/mediainhome/children/rep3.pdf

Masterman, L. (1997). A rationale for media education. In R. Kubey (Ed.), *Media literacy in the information age: Current perspectives, information and behavior* (Vol. 6, pp. 15–68). New Brunswick, NJ: Transaction.

Messaris, P. (1998). Visual aspects of media literacy. *Journal of Communication, 48,* 70–80.

Meyrowitz, J. (1998). Multiple media literacies. *Journal of Communication, 48,* 96–108.

Silverblatt, A. (1995). *Media literacy: Keys to interpreting media messages.* Westport, CT: Praeger.

Policy and Law

Just as parents and schools have an important role in the relationship of children and teens to mass media through mediation and media literacy, so too does the government play a role through the development of laws and policies that can enable more quality media opportunities for children in their homes.

From the early history of the relationship of children and the media, many have personal stories to tell, but some, such as U.S. Representative Edward Markey of Massachusetts, were in a position to try to make changes in their roles as policymakers. Markey played an important role in both the CTA and V-chip legislation. He most recently sponsored a bill to provide a government subdomain on the Internet for children. He explained why he pursued legislation on children and media in the following account.

A Copycat Crime As Told by Rep. Markey

As a young state representative in 1975, I was ... alarmed by a very tragic event involving the interaction of television and children. A television program was broadcast that portrayed a gang of young toughs pouring gasoline on a homeless man and burning him alive. The next day on the streets of Boston, a gang of young toughs poured gasoline on a homeless man and burned him alive.

When our local broadcaster attempted to blame the network for the decision to air the show, I went on the program to point out that local general managers of TV stations have the legal right to reject programming that they consider too violent for their local community and, therefore, cannot escape responsibility by pointing their finger up the chain of distribution. But the fact remains that most general managers never exercise that right on behalf of families and children. That is why, over the years, I have searched for ways of giving parents the power, through technology, to affect programming decisions that historically have been made by TV executives and advertisers with little regard to their impact on the welfare of small children. (Markey, 1998)[1]

[1]From address to the Second World Summit on Television and Children, London, by E. Markey. Copyright by E. Markey. Reprinted with permission.

We also see how other groups contribute to policy, including the roles of the FCC as presented by Commissioner Susan Ness, the FTC, advocacy groups such as ACT and The Center for Media Education, and media industries. Legislation as well as recommendations for future policy are considered.

The legislation that had been considered from the early days of television took several decades due to the conflict in rights with the First Amendment. The free speech of broadcasters took precedence over the public interest of the protection of children.

THE FIRST AMENDMENT

Print Standard

The First Amendment has several standards and has been interpreted differently for different media. The strongest First Amendment standard is the one for the print media. Print, of course, was the dominant mass medium when the First Amendment was written in the 18th century. The print media could be owned by anyone who could afford a printing press.

Broadcast Standard

Because of the publicly owned airwaves, the situation for broadcasters differed from the printing press, which required no publicly owned resources and needed no government regulation. When radio broadcasters wanted help from the government due to the chaos of early radio, the Radio Act of 1927 established the public interest standard to allow regulation in spite of the First Amendment. The public interest standard states that to get a license to use the public airwaves, the broadcaster must operate in the public interest. The public interest standard for broadcasters began with the Radio Act of 1927 and continued in the Communications Act of 1934 with the establishment of the FCC to regulate broadcasters. The broadcasters have perhaps the least freedom because of the public nature of the airwaves. Both radio and television operators have resisted the regulation of the FCC.

The public interest standard was based on the fact that the airwaves belong to the people and the government could manage them to serve the people. There are at least two ways to view the public interest: egalitarian and libertarian. The egalitarian mode allows for regulation to guarantee that people are well served by the publicly owned resource. The libertarian mode sees the public interest as a function of the marketplace and is simply what the public is interested in (Minow & LaMay, 1995).

Minow and LaMay (1995) took an egalitarian view of the public interest standard, which they said can support free speech and serve children:

The choice is not between free speech and the marketplace on the one hand, and governmental censorship and bureaucracy on the other. The choice is to serve the needs of children and use the opportunities presented by the superhighway in the digital age to enrich their lives. If we turn away from that choice, the consequences of our inaction will be even greater educational neglect, more craven and deceptive consumerism, and inappropriate levels of sex and violence—a wasteland vaster than anyone can imagine, or would care to. (p. 15)

Thus Minow returned to the *vast wasteland* phrase he made famous in describing television in 1961 (see chapter 5).

Cable and Internet Standards

Another medium using public resources is the cable medium. Cable operators use rights of way to lay their cables either on poles or in the ground. However, the Cable Act of 1984 does not restrict cablecasters as much as broadcasters. In fact, the cable operators have a First Amendment standard closer to the print standard. Cable operators have some regulations from their individual franchises, but those regulations are not content regulations and cablecasters may choose to put whatever they want on their channels.

The standard for Internet First Amendment rights still is in flux, but it seems that Internet operators have First Amendment rights similar to the print media. Whereas some may see the media operator's First Amendment rights conflicting with the public interest standard as seen in legislation to protect children, others like Minow and LaMay (1995) see them working hand in hand.

PUBLIC PRESSURE

Much of the public concern with children and media has to do with sex and violence. Congressional hearings on television violence began as early as 1954 and continued for some 35 years before the CTA of 1990. What did they accomplish? Cooper (1996) said the hearings served both the Congress and the broadcasters in a public relations way:

> Wishing to appear responsive to the concern of the viewers, parents, and citizen advocacy groups, Congress employed the "raised eyebrow" method of regulation to reduce television violence. Through these hearings, and the subsequent media coverage, Congress brought concerns over television violence to the public arena and forced broadcasters to take some action or risk appearing indifferent to the public's concern. (p. 138)

In addition, to the extent that broadcasters appeared to be acting for viewers, broadcasters benefited (Cooper, 1996). Public relations were important here because the public was putting pressure on Congress to act. Advocacy groups such as ACT, under the leadership of Peggy Charren, did not rest until the CTA was passed in 1990. ACT worked with the FCC, the FTC, and Congress for 30 years as advocates for good media for children (Kunkel, 1990).

THE FCC AND ACT IN THE 1970S

ACT brought the parental concerns about the effects of television and concerns about improving the quality of children's television first to the FCC in 1970. In 1974, the FCC issued the Children's Television Report and Policy Statement that established, at least in writing, that broadcasters have some responsibilities to children. The document recognized that most broadcast stations were not providing adequate service for children. This lack of service was linked to the broadcaster's requirement of fulfilling the public interest standard to use the public airwaves. In their report the FCC called for reform in children's programming and advertising. However, this FCC action was in the form of guidelines, which provided standards to be used to evaluate stations for license renewal. Compliance was voluntary (Kunkel, 1990).

Deregulation in the 1980s and Advertising

The battle lines were drawn between the broadcasters who wanted no FCC requirements and children's advocates. Continuing their efforts to avoid harmful effects and gain quality programming for children, ACT in the late 1970s next turned their attention to the FTC, a group that could deal with concerns about too much advertising. ACT "petitioned the FTC to ban commercials on all children's programs" (Minow & LaMay, 1995, p. 50).

The early 1980s brought a different view of regulation to Congress and the era of deregulation began under President Ronald Reagan: "In 1980 Congress stripped the FTC of the power to rule on 'unfair' advertising practices" (Minow & LaMay, 1995, p. 51). During deregulation, the protection of the public interest obligation was lost and the libertarian model of letting the marketplace decide took over. In 1982 and 1983, the FCC decided to take off of the books all requirements with regard to local broadcasters' responsibility to the children's television market as part of the Reagan administration's deregulation philosophy. By 1988 and 1989, children's television programming had dropped precipitously as a percentage of the total week's schedule on the average local television station (E. Markey, personal communication, February 29, 2000).

During this era there was less programming for children and what there was seemed to many like a program-length commercial because the same characters in the program also were promoted in the commercials. Development of the children's audience with program-length commercials and without the enforced protection of a public interest obligation was problematic in the 1980s:

The idea of children as a "special" audience, thought historically important in American culture, simply cannot be supported in an economic system that allows no consideration for public service. Government agencies, instituted to assure that the broadcasting industries would serve the public, have become increasingly dominated by industry. And commercial-length programs are the "logical" extension of a system that weds commerce and entertainment, with little regard for "the public interest, convenience, and necessity." (Pecora, 1998, p. 155)

The industries being referred to are the cable and broadcast television programming industries, as well as the advertising and toy industries.

The deregulation approach was based on a marketplace that includes the many channels of cable television. However, all homes and all children did not have cable television. Markey said as much as 30% of children do not have access to cable television: "Those children tend to come from the lower socio-economic backgrounds and free over the air broadcasting is still the only way in which those children can gain access to the educational and informational programming, which television has the potential of supplying" (E. Markey, personal communication, February 29, 2000). Research and public pressure following deregulation under President Reagan in the 1980s created a lot of pressure for some kind of legislation. Markey said the CTA of 1990 was a direct result of that deregulation because deregulation resulted in much less children's television programming.

The Role of Research

Although Cooper (1996) concluded the hearings were mostly a public relations tool, she did say that benefits included funding for research. Television effects research funded by Congress, and the Surgeon General's investigation in particular, funneled millions of dollars to research projects and contributed to the growth of communication research. These studies helped legitimize communication research and acted as a catalyst for a discipline of social science research that continues to flourish today (Cooper, 1996). As we see later, that same public pressure has led to legislation that could not pass Constitutional muster on the issue of indecency and efforts to protect children from online pornography.

THE CTA OF 1990

As the ranking Democrat on the House Telecommunications Subcommittee and with the Democrats holding a majority in Congress in 1990, Markey chaired that committee. Markey said two legal factors allowed the CTA of 1990 to happen:

The fact that broadcasters use public spectrum ... makes it easier to pass laws that mandate certain types of speech by broadcasters that is impossible to be imposed upon other media. Secondly, the fact that we're talking about the children's marketplace also puts it into a historically protected special category that the Supreme

Court has always allowed to be treated differently than if the Congress is speaking about an adult audience. (E. Markey, personal communication, February 29, 2000)

Under Markey's leadership, the CTA passed Congress in 1990. The consensus was historic and provided a framework for children's television that included a mandate for children's programming and a limit on advertising.

> It is the first such legislation in the 40 years of television broadcasting in this country. It establishes the principle that broadcasters have a social responsibility to their child audiences. The advantage to the approach used in this legislation is that it avoids the thorny issues of censorship. It specifies a positive requirement that programming meet the needs of children rather than a restriction on what may be broadcast. (Huston et al., 1992, p. 123)

The act was implemented January 1, 1992, passing without President George Bush's signature:

> First, it established that each station must provide educational and informational programming for children (but in no specific amount) in order to qualify for license renewal. Second, it limited advertising during children's programs to no more than 12 minutes per hour on weekdays, 10.5 minutes per hour on weekends. (Kunkel, 1990, p. 279)

The FCC's Role

After the CTA, the next step was to develop regulations that would support it, and that job went to the FCC. FCC Commissioner Susan Ness was on board to help write the FCC regulations in 1996. She described the FCC role this way: "Where Congress has taken specific steps, such as with the Children's Television Act of 1990, we have an obligation to fulfill those roles. We do so from a regulatory perspective. So we have a regulatory role to play as far as implementing the Children's Television Act" (S. Ness, personal communication, March 2, 2000). The CTA had a specific number of minutes for advertising limits, but programming had no specifications:

> The programming requirements were so loose that it was difficult to prove that the broadcaster was not meeting his obligations. And so we undertook, beginning in '94, ending in '96, to come up with appropriate regulations to put meat on the bones of that extremely important act. (S. Ness, personal communication, March 2, 2000)

Just as ACT played a role in getting the CTA passed, another advocacy group helped to give notice that the CTA was not being enforced. In 1992 The Center for Media Education (CME) did a study with Georgetown University School of Law's Institute for Public Representation titled *A Report on Station Compliance with the Children's Television Act.*

CME documented that stations were re-labeling old reruns such as *The Jetsons, The Flintstones,* and *Leave it to Beaver* as "educational." (*The Jetsons* was described by one station as an educational program that "teaches children what life will be like in the 21st Century.") Other stations claimed that raunchy afternoon talk shows were serving educational needs. "FCC-friendly" programs, as the TV industry called them, were often scheduled in pre-dawn time slots when few people were likely to be watching. (CME, 2000)

The study prompted the FCC to take another view and they found that further regulations were needed.

Information and Feedback Via the FCC Web Page.   However, the issue of program content regulation runs directly counter to the First Amendment. Therefore, the FCC in their 1996 rules stepped around the First Amendment by giving parents a way to check on their local broadcasters and talk directly with them and the FCC. They set up a Web page, thus using technology to facilitate pressure from the public for educational programming. The FCC encouraged broadcasters to file reports showing their compliance with the CTA online so parents could see them and communicate with the broadcaster about their efforts at creating children's programming (Children's Educational Television, 2002). The FCC encouraged broadcasters to report their educational and informational shows directly online.

> Such information will assist parents who wish to guide their children's television viewing and, if large numbers of parents use that information to choose educational programming for their children, increase the likelihood that the market will respond with more educational programming. In addition, better information should help parents and others have an effective dialogue with broadcasters in their community about children's programming and, where appropriate, to urge programming improvements without resorting to government intervention. (FCC, 1996, paragraph 3)

How well the Web page is working has not yet been evaluated.

Defining Educational and Core Programming.   Second, the FCC had to take the word *educational* and make it more concrete so that *The Jetsons* need not apply. Again, however, the restriction on content regulation had to be bypassed. In their reporting of compliance, broadcasters were required to explain how the programming they claimed fulfilled their licensing obligation was educational. "Educational and informational television programming is any television programming that furthers the educational and informational needs of children 16 years of age and under in any respect, including the child's intellectual/cognitive or social/emotional needs" (47 U.S.C. 154, 303, 334. 2. Section 73.671 paragraph c.). Ness explained the inclusion of social and emotional needs:

Sometimes the most important lessons children can learn are lessons that involve their emotional well-being. They may not sit through or be interested in yet another class on math on a Saturday morning or Sunday or after school. But the lessons they may very well have learned if it's properly structured, if the program really has educational content, typically if educators have been instrumental in putting it together from day one, not a tagline or message at the end but rather a really meaningful program, that can be an educational program. We wanted to make sure that was a possibility. There are a number of those types of programs on. I've watched some of them and, judging as a parent, I would find these programs to be very helpful and educational and geared towards children and geared toward specific age kids. (S. Ness, personal communication, March 2, 2000)

So the programming must teach cognitive and affective lessons in a purposeful way. The FCC referred to educational and informational programming as *core programming* and extended the definition to include various criteria that help define the core programming:

(1) (Core programming) has serving the educational and informational needs of children ages 16 and under as a significant purpose; (2) It is aired between the hours of 7:00 a.m. and 10:00 p.m.; (3) It is a regularly scheduled weekly program; (4) It is at least 30 minutes in length; (5) The educational and informational objective and the target child audience are specified in writing in the licensee's Children's Television Programming Report, ... and (6) Instructions for listing the program as educational/informational, including an indication of the age group for which the program is intended, are provided by the licensee to publishers of program guides. (47 U.S.C. 154, 303, 334. 2. Section 73.671 paragraph c.)

These criteria are in response to the behavior of the broadcasters described earlier as well as in response to advocates who had lobbied for these specific and objective criteria.

Enforcement of Regulations.   The device that is most likely to get the attention of the broadcaster, however, is the requirements that are tied to the nonrenewal of licenses for use of the airwaves. In the case of the FCC regulations for the CTA, those requirements are the 3-hour rule and the advertising minutes.

The whole point of the CTA was to get more educational programming. Although 3 hours a week is not a lot, it is a fixed amount that can be measured. What happens if it is less than 3 hours a week? The FCC in the report seemed to bend over backward to go to the issue of intent and to say that the they could meet the requirement if "they air a package of programming that demonstrates a level of commitment to educating and informing children that is at least equivalent to airing three hours per week of core programming" (FCC, 1996, Introduction, paragraph 5).

More quantifiable and thus more useful in ruling on nonrenewal of licenses is the measure of advertising minutes. As of 1995, noncompliance with measures of advertising minutes resulted in fines. In particular, KTTU-TV in Tucson, Arizona, and WSEE-TV in Erie, Pennsylvania, were fined $125,000 and $100,000, respectively, for surpassing the ad limits for children's television. In addition, both stations got 2-year short-term renewals in addition to the fines (Craig & Smith, 1996, Administration of the Act, paragraph 1).

Is the CTA Working?

With regulations in place, several perspectives can be presented to answer the question, "Is the CTA working?" According to Markey, the answer is yes:

> It's substantially improved over where it was in 1990 and '95 when the regulations would have begun to be implemented. But having the law on the books gives the public interest community the club or coercion they need to continue to put the pressure on the slower broadcasters to measure up to the national standard. (E. Markey, personal communication, February 29, 2000)

FCC Commissioner Ness agreed with Markey, saying that the number of commercial minutes has gone down and the quality has gone up. If the broadcasters do not comply with the limits on ads, they are fined. Regarding the amount of educational programming, Ness said she sees substantial improvement in the objective factors such as number of hours, regularity, and time of day. She said she had no objective evaluation of quality of programming. Instead she reported what some programmers have said to her: "A number of programmers have said our actions were critical and that they actually were given an opportunity to have their programs aired" (S. Ness, personal communication, March 2, 2000). Children's programmers may be happy, but reports from broadcasters are less positive.

In a survey conducted by Craig and Smith (1999) regarding the responses of Michigan broadcasters, the majority of broadcasters who responded reported no change in amount of children's programming due to the 3-hour rule. Factors included the response that the stations had been carrying children's programming before the rules. One response was: "Stations with large segments of kid's programming didn't have to change a lot. Those who did just found some E / I [education and information programming] and placed it in less desirable time periods" (p. 17). Those who said the 3-hour rule had been effective were in the minority. One such response was: "There are more educational programs available in syndication and on the networks so the quality of programming has improved. The FCC has also done various spot checks to make sure stations are complying and I don't think any station owner wants to pay fines for non-compliance" (p. 17). Craig and Smith concluded that the child audience was being spread out over a larger number of stations, thus lessening incentive in the form of ratings by any individual broadcaster. In addition, many of the children were migrating to cable, where the quality of children's programming is better because they can focus on a smaller audience share and specialize in that market, as does Nickelodeon.

As the broadcasters continue to resist any incursions, some critics find that the CTA has intruded on the First Amendment rights of broadcasters and call the regulations beginning with CTA "a new censorship." Maines (1996) argued that the CTA, the V-chip legislation, and the Communications Decency Act amount to a "new censorship" and called the CTA, "arguably the most intrusive law in the history of television" (paragraph 25). The "new censorship" laws are characterized by a rationale that offers ways to protect children and may be unconstitutional. However, both the CTA and V-chip have not been challenged by the courts.

THE V-CHIP

Whereas the CTA tried to encourage good-quality TV, the Telecommunications Act of 1996 included sections that tried to exclude bad-quality television. Whereas the CTA applies only to broadcast television, the V-chip applies to cable as well.

> So it's not enough you just put on good stuff. You also want to give parents the ability to block out things they don't want their kids to see. And that's where the V-chip comes in. It's using technology in a way that gives parents the ability to customize their TV set for their own child. (E.. Markey, personal communication, February 29, 2000)

FIG. 9.1. Some families want to block violence on their televisions as Christian Incandalla, age 9, illustrates. The government has provided a way to block by requiring V-chips in televisions. Reprinted with permission.

For children, protection was sought through a device called the V-chip, or violence chip. There are many devices that can block certain programs, but the V-chip is embedded in the television itself. For some, the V-chip sounds like censorship. Maines (1996) saw the legislation as beyond a "slippery slope" and called it a "cliff." By accepting the advisories and other regulation, he said industry accepts government regulation of content. Maines said the legislation would not work; for example, no one would use the V-chip and no one would watch the educational programs. He also said adults would not accept restricting speech to what is appropriate for children. However, Markey disagreed that the V-chip constitutes censorship:

> The V-chip technology in and of itself has no ability to censor. The decision as to whether or not a program is seen by a child is made by the mother and the father in the same way that a parent would decide whether a salesman at the front door would get into the living room to sell a product that a child might not benefit from. So I analogized the V-chip to the safety cap on a bottle of aspirin, to a seat belt in an automobile. In and of itself it's not sufficient for a parent to protect their child. The parent also should make sure the bottle of aspirin is up on the top shelf where the kids can't reach it, that the parent drives safely when they're in the car, or that the parent be an otherwise all around good parent as well. (E. Markey, personal communication, February 29, 2000)

Like the FCC's use of a Web page to encourage communication between the viewer and the broadcaster in its 1996 rules, Congress passed V-chip legislation that used technology as a tool to allow parents to control what came into their homes. The V-chip legislation was part of the Telecommunications Act of 1996 (Public Law 104-104) called "Parental Choice in Television Programming" (FCC, n.d.-a). Congress "prescribed procedures for Establishment of a Television Rating Code" and "prescribed procedures for newly manufactured television sets to include a mechanism to block programs, referred to popularly as the V-Chip."

From there, the FCC set out rules that established specific guidelines and deadlines: "All sets 13 inches or larger manufactured after January 1, 2000 must have V-Chip technology" (FCC, n.d.-b). Set-top boxes for older sets are also available. The ratings can help to determine what is blocked by the V-chip. The technology for the V-chip is similar to closed captioning. However, whereas closed captioning increases the size of the audience to include the hearing impaired by providing the text of what is being said on the screen, the V-chip may decrease the audience by blocking channels or programs (McDowell & Maitland, 1998).

RATINGS FOR TELEVISION

The television industry determined the specifics of the ratings system that allows parents to block out programs via V-chip or monitor children for some types of programs. The cooperation of the broadcast television industry with the voluntary ratings was based on several factors. The movie industry has had an age-based ratings system for many years. Cable television also already had a system. Foreign government departments recommended the ratings for their use: "Programs encoded with violence ratings could be seen as offering an extra value-added component, reducing some of the cultural frictions associated with television program exports" (McDowell & Maitland, 1998, p. 411).

Age-Based Ratings

With the help of the Motion Picture Association of America (MPAA), the television industry began with age-based ratings in January 1997. The voluntary age category included the following: "TV-Y (suitable for all children), TV-Y7 (for children over age 7), TV-G (suitable for all audiences), TV-PG (unsuitable for younger children), TV-14 (unsuitable for children under age 14), and TV-M (unsuitable for children under age 17)" (Sneegas & Plank, 1998, p. 425). The TV-Y designation indicates that the program is for children ages 2 through 6 and is not expected to frighten younger children. TV-Y7 indicates children younger than 7 might be frightened by the content. The designation also reflects a developmental point, as children younger than 7 cannot differentiate fantasy from reality. Children older than 7 can judge that difference and these shows are more appropriate for these older children. The rest of the designations are designed for the entire audience, adults as well as children. TV-G rating is not designed for children. Although the child may watch unattended, this rating does not guarantee the absence of inappropriate messages (see study on G rating later). TV-PG indicates parents may want to watch with their children. For TV-14, parents are strongly cautioned that the material may be unsuitable for children younger than 14. TV-MA indicates programming designed for adults and unsuitable for children under 17.

The MPAA has used the age-based ratings for films since the 1960s. A recent study in the *Journal of the American Medical Association* indicated that G-rated animated films do contain violence (Associated Press, 2000, p. 15). One problem with film ratings is that they label what is offensive rather than what is harmful. A second problem is that sex is rated as more offensive than violence. Third, the ratings look at amount of sex or violence instead of context "such as how realistic it is, the rewards and punishments associated with the violent act, and the degree of justification for the violence" (Donnerstein, Slaby, & Eron, 1998, p. 244).

Content-Based Ratings

Child advocacy organizations were not satisfied with age-based ratings and worked to get content-based ratings included. In October 1998, with some holdouts including NBC (broadcast TV) and BET (cable TV), the television industry began using revised guidelines including content description warnings indicated by the letters S, V, L, and D. S designates sexual content, V violence, L language, and D suggestive dialogue. In addition, FV identifies fantasy violence for children older than 7 years of age. Neither news nor sports are rated ("National PTA," 1997). When coupled with age designations, the L ratings may indicate coarse language for the TV-PG rating and strong coarse language for the TV-14 designation. (For Web sites explaining ratings, see "Resources on the Web.")

Although ratings can be a helpful tool and can help parents use the V-chip to block out programming they do not want their children to watch, parents need to be aware that the ratings are insufficient protection and are not a substitute for parental supervision.

> No one has challenged the V-chip in the courts. Markey explained why: I think the reason the V-chip was never challenged in court was that the broadcasters knew they would lose. It would be impossible for them to argue a technology in and of itself was censoring any information. Each family controls the technology and as a result the First Amendment right of free speech of the families also (is exercised). (E. Markey, personal communication, February 29, 2000)

The ways children respond to ratings differ by gender, according to research. Thus parental guidance can play a critical role.

Research on Ratings

Research on television ratings indicates that girls seem to respond in the way intended for ratings due to *the tainted fruit* effect, but boys seem to respond with what is called *the forbidden fruit* effect, and they are attracted to shows labeled inappropriate for them. In addition to the gender difference, there are age differences. Children ages 9 to 11 are attracted to forbidden fruit as well (Sneegas & Plank, 1998). Research on how parents use television ratings "confirms initial reports by the Annenberg Public Policy Center that a relatively small proportion of parents actively incorporate TV ratings into their mediation of television" (Abelman, 1999, p. 544). Abelman surveyed parents of second graders and found that those who needed the ratings the most did not use them:

> They tend to believe that television does not necessarily have significant positive or negative effects on children. When mediation is enacted by these parents, it tends to be highly unfocused. Contrary to predictions, the children of these low mediators are the heaviest consumers of television in the sample. They also tend to be boys. (Abelman, 1999, p. 545)

Because parents who need the ratings the least are most likely to use them, Abelman (1999) said the MPAA is "preaching to the choir" (p. 544). Other media, including the movie, music, and game industries, also have adopted ratings.

RATINGS OF MOVIES, MUSIC, AND GAME INDUSTRIES

The FTC was directed to study the ratings provided by the movie, music, and game industries. The original FTC report in 2000 found that the movie, music, and game industries all market violence to children while rating their messages as appropriate for children, thus misleading parents.

The Senate Commerce Committee requested two follow-up reports. The report finding was that progress had been made in some areas including providing rating information in advertising for the movie, music, and game industries. In particular, the report found no R-rated movie ads in magazines marketed to teens or in trailers of movies shown before G- or PG-rated movies. However, R-rated movie trailers were available to teens on television and often reasons for ratings were not readable in the advertising. The music industry made no change in their practices. The parental advisory labeling program is different from the ratings for other media in that it does not designate an age when the music is inappropriate or reasons why it is inappropriate. However, the music industry did improve in providing the parental guidance information in advertising. The electronic gaming industry has progressed by providing new standards for "limiting ads for M-rated games where children constitute a certain percentage of the audience: 35 percent for television and radio and 45 percent for print and the Internet" (FTC, 2001, p. iii). Although they did not advertise on television, there were some violent M-rated games advertised in children's media including magazines and Web sites.

Part of the report is a "mystery" shopper survey that checked to see if retailers were enforcing the restrictions, for example, by checking identification for those purchasing tickets to R-rated movies. The report found few changes since the last survey with "nearly half (48 percent) of the theaters (selling) tickets to R-rated movies to the underage moviegoers, while 90 percent of the music retailers sold explicit content recordings to the underage shoppers" (FTC, 2001, pp. iii–iv).

INTERNET PROTECTION FROM INDECENCY UNCONSTITUTIONAL

The Communications Decency Act (CDA) and two other acts that have attempted to restrict indecency on the Internet have been shot down by the courts. Like the V-chip, this act was designed to exclude programming that was not acceptable for children on cable and the Internet. However, the CDA also made it illegal for adults to access information on sexual topics. The Court found in 1997 for the first time that the First Amendment standard for the Internet is most like the standard for print media. Once the CDA was found unconstitutional in 1997 for the Internet provision, the Congress made another attempt to regulate the Internet with the Child Online Protection Act (COPA) passed in 1998. COPA replaced CDA and is referred to as CDA II. The Congress addressed the faults the court found in the CDA and made the new act narrower in its applications, trying to recreate the successful *community standard* found in the *Miller v. California* case that still is used today to evaluate decency for broadcast media.

COPA differs from CDA in that it only applies to Web communications. Second, only communications for commercial purposes are affected. Third, the COPA applies to communications that are harmful to minors (Miller, 1999).

> CDA II uses Miller v. California as a model to try to identify indecent material. However, the federal appeals court (The Third Circuit Court of Appeals) that began looking at the case in November 1999 questioned the term "community standard" because the Internet goes worldwide. The judges feared that the most conservative standard might become the "community standard." (Flagg, 1999)

In June 2000, the Third Circuit Court of Appeals found COPA unconstitutional "because it is impossible to establish one 'community standard' by which Internet speech can be governed" ("Late Bulletins," 2000).

The government tried a third time in 2000 to ban indecency on the Internet with the Children's Internet Protection Act (CIPA). The approach for this act was to require filtering at libraries to protect children as they access the Internet at school and in public libraries. The CIPA required libraries to use filtering software to continue receiving government funding. "Under CIPA, no school or library may receive discounts unless it certifies that it is enforcing a policy of Internet safety that includes the use of filtering or blocking technology" (Universal Service Administration Company, n.d.). The libraries argued that would deprive their patrons of their First Amendment rights. A federal court sided with libraries, Web site publishers, and the American Civil Liberties Union to reject CIPA, Congress's third attempt at protecting children from the dangers of the Internet. Restrictions for schools still apply. The U.S. District Court agreed with the libraries ("Children's Internet Protection Act Struck Down," 2002). Both COPA and CIPA are being appealed.

Like other structural ways of honoring the First Amendment while protecting children such as the V-Chip, the fourth try at protecting children from indecency on the Internet came in the 2002 Dot-Kids Implementation and Efficiency Act. This law provides a separate place on the Internet for Children's Web sties. Children under 13 would be served by a dot-kids domain managed by NeuStar. Of course, this management of the Web would only apply to the dot-us site, not other sites. Regulations include prohibition of hyperlinks directing users outside the dot-kids domain. In addition, there will be no chat rooms or interpersonal communication without site sponsor guarantee of monitoring due to risks such as pedophiles (Minkel, 2003). While the act is less likely to have its constitutionality challenged, it does not protect children using the rest o the Internet domains.

ALTERNATIVES TO LEGISLATION ON INTERNET INDECENCY

Alexander (2002) argued that Congress has passed the three acts to try to protect children from indecency due to political pressures from their constituency, knowing the acts would not be found to be constitutional. He concluded that the problems must be solved by those closest to them at the local level including parents, schools, and libraries. He suggested three components: "(1) filtration; (2) acceptable use policies; and (3) monitoring" (p. 1023). He saw Congress's job as to "facilitate and encourage," not mandate (p. 1023).

He recommended Congress work with the computer industry to develop standards for home PCs and software to be sold with filters turned on. This suggestion makes a different presumption; that is, the filter must be turned off for adult use rather than turned on for children's use. Alexander also suggested that the government provide tools for parents such as the FBI's *A Parent's Guide to Internet Safety*. Schools need monitoring and acceptable use policies that the government can help with. Libraries should develop their policies based on community standards. States can provide advice and enforcement once community standards have been developed. For example, Utah has a "'porn czar' who can oversee prosecutions of those who violate community standards" (Alexander, 2002, p. 1025).

In addition, Internet service providers (ISPs) can provide their own filtering and acceptable use policies. "The filtering software serves as the hook and the window into a filtered family-friendly cybercommunity" (Alexander, 2002, p. 1029). Self-regulation like that the MPAA provides could work for the ISPs as well.

THE QUESTION OF PRIVACY ON THE INTERNET

The federal government has been more successful in providing legislation to protect children from invasions of privacy than protection from indecency. The COPPA protects the privacy of children under the age of 13. It became law in 1998 and the FTC regulations have been in effect since April 2000. COPPA focuses on children's privacy and how Web sites gather information about children without their understanding or knowledge:

> Generally, the COPPA requires that the operator of a children's Web site that collects personal information must provide notice on the site of what information is collected and how the information is used. Second, the Web site operator must obtain verifiable parental consent for the collection, use or disclosure of personal information from children. (Hertzel, 2000, pp. 437–438)

Getting parental consent can be a costly process, especially for small to medium-sized Web providers. The FTC gave more specific procedures for obtaining parental consent. Because of cost concerns, the FTC provided a sliding scale, which allows an operator to use varying consent mechanisms depending on how the information collected will be used. For example, the scale allows a Web site that collects personal information from a child to verify consent via e-mail only if the information is used for internal purposes. However, the Web operator must take additional steps to substantiate the parent's identity. For instance, the Web site operator may phone or send a letter to the parent confirming his or her identity:

> For a Web site operator that plans to disclose collected information to a third party or post the collected information in general areas such as chat rooms or bulletin boards, the operator must use more rigorous means to obtain consent such as requiring credit card verification. (Hertzel, 2000, p. 442)

In addition to the legislative options such as the COPPA, the Online Privacy Alliance (OPA) provides some self-regulation by the industry. OPA is a "coalition of Internet industry groups ... created to deal directly with online privacy issues" (Hertzel, 2000, p. 444). Another alternative to government regulation is filtering software, which gives parents some control over what their children can access on the Web (Hertzel, 2000).

SUMMARY

The development of government laws and regulations for children and media has focused on four themes:

1. Encouraging quality programming with limited advertising (CTA).
2. Giving parents tools to control what they judge to be harmful programming (V-chip and access to broadcast compliance reports on the Internet).
3. Attempting to limit children's exposure to indecent materials that are aimed at children (CDA, COPA, CIPA).
4. Attempting to protect the privacy of children as they use the Internet (COPPA).

These laws and regulations have been developed through the work and interaction of several groups including parents and child advocacy groups such as ACT and CME, U.S. Representatives such as Ed Markey, FCC Commissioners such as Susan Ness, the FTC, and the courts. The development of these laws involve the special place children have in the development of laws, but the courts also protect the First Amendment rights of adults. In doing so, they look to the special aspects of each medium and develop a First Amendment standard based on the attributes of each medium. The challenge is to protect children without restricting the rights of adults.

FOR FURTHER CONSIDERATION

1. Choose two mass media and explain how their First Amendment standards differ.

2. Choose one of the groups that play a role in the development of law and policy and explain how their role has been seen in the history of children's media legislation.

3. Choose one of the issues in children's mass media law (see Summary) and explain how that issue has been addressed in legislation.

4. Choose one of the preceding recommendations or offer one from your readings or from your own ideas to explain and support in an essay. How might your recommendation be accomplished?

RESOURCES ON THE WEB

- FCC Web site for Children's Television Act: http://svartifoss2.fcc.gov/prod/kidvid/prod/kidvid.htm
- FCC Web site for checking compliance by local broadcaster for the Children's Television Act: http://svartifoss2.fcc.gov/prod/kidvid/prod/kidvid.htm
- FBI Web site for *A Parent's Guide to Internet Safety:* http://www.fbi.gov/publications/pguide/pguidee.htm
- Ratings Web sites: The Classification and Rating Administration (CARA) gives ratings for all media at www.parentalguide.org. "With this Web site, the entertainment industry has come together to provide a central resource for parents and caregivers seeking more information about these guidelines." The film site, sponsored by the MPAA, for example, is linked to the CARA Web site. It has its own Web address, which is http://www.filmratings.com. The database includes movies rated since 1968! Other links include the Entertainment Software Rating Board, The National Association of Broadcasters, the National Cable Television Association, the Recording Industry Association of America, and TV Parental Guidelines. Other ratings sites for parents include http://www.kids-in-mind.com and http://www.screenit.com.

REFERENCES

Abelman, R. (1999). Preaching to the choir: Profiling TV advisory ratings users. *Journal of Broadcasting and Electronic Media, 43,* 529–550.

Alexander, M. C. (2002, Summer). The First Amendment and problems of political viability: The case of Internet pornography. *Harvard Journal of Law & Public Policy, 25,* 977–1030. Retrieved July 24, 2002 from EBSCOhost.

Associated Press. (2000, May 24). Study cites violence in "G" cartoon flicks. *The Keene Sentinel,* p. 15.

Center for Media Education. (2000). *A field guide to the Children's Television Act.* Retrieved March 6, 2000 from http://www.cme.org

Children's Educational Television: The FCC's Children's Television Web page. Reviewed and updated April 3, 2002. Retrieved July 29, 2002 at http://svartifoss2.fcc.gov/prod/kidvid/prod/kidvid.htm

Children's Internet Protection Act struck down. (2002, August). *The Computer & Internet Lawyer, 19(8)*, 8.

Cooper, C. (1996). *Violence on television, Congressional inquiry, public criticism, and industry response: A policy analysis.* Lanham, MD: University Press of America.

Craig, J. R., & Smith, B. R. (1996, December). The Children's Television Act to date: A market survey. *Communications and the Law, 18*, 4. Retrieved July 24, 2002, from EBSCOhost.

Craig, J. R., & Smith, B. R. (1999, Winter). Implementing the FCC's three-hour children's television rule: A first look. *Feedback, 40*, 14–19.

Donnerstein, E., Slaby, R. G., & Eron, L. D. (1994). The mass media and youth aggression. In L. D. Eron, J. H. Gentry, & P. Schlegel (Eds), *A reason to hope: A psychosocial perspective on violence and youth* (pp. 219–250). Washington, DC: American Psychological Association.

FCC. (1996, August 8). *Policies and rules concerning children's television programming* (FCC 96-335). Retrieved May 2000 from http://www.fcc.gov/bureaus/mass_media/orders/1996/fcc96335.txt

FCC (n.d.-a). Parental choice in television programming: Excerpts from V-chip legislation. Retrieved May 24, 2000 from http://www.fcc.gov/vchip/legislation.html

FCC. (n.d.-b) V-chip home page. Retrieved May 9, 2000 from http://www.fcc.gov/vchip

Federal Trade Commission. (2001, December). *Marketing violent entertainment to children: A one-year follow-up review of industry practices in the motion picture, music recording & electronic game industries: A report to Congress.* Retrieved July 24, 2002 from www.ftc.gov/os/2001/12/violencereport1.pdf

Flagg, G. (1999, December). Judges question COPA Constitutionality. *American Libraries, 30*, 12. Retrieved May 30, 2000 from EBSCOhost.

Hertzel, D. A. (2000). Don't talk to strangers: An analysis of government and industry efforts to protect a child's privacy online. *Federal Communications Law Journal, 52*, 429–451.

Huston, A. C., Donnerstein, E., Fairchild, H., Feshbach, N. D., Katz, P., Murray, J. P., et al. (1992). *Big world, small screen: The role of television in American society.* Lincoln: University of Nebraska Press.

Kunkel, D. (1990). Child and family television regulatory policy. In J. Bryant (Ed.), *Television and the American family* (pp. 349–368). Hillsdale, NJ: Lawrence Erlbaum Associates.

Late bulletins. (2000, July). *Library Journal, 125*, 11. Retrieved August 1, 2000, from EBSCOhost.

Maines, P. D. (1996, September 14). The new censorship. *Editor & Publisher.* Retrieved July 24, 2002 from EBSCOhost.

Markey, E. J. (1998, March 10). Address to the Second World Summit on Television and Children, London.

McDowell, S. D., & Maitland, C. (1998). The V-chip in Canada and the United States: Themes and variations in design and deployment. *Journal of Broadcasting and Electronic Media, 42*, 401–422.

Miller, H. L. (1999, December). Strike two: An analysis of the Child Online Protection Act's constitutional failures. *Federal Communications Law Journal, 52*, 155–188.

Minkel, W. (2003, January). Bush signs Dot-Kids into law. *School Library Journal, 49* [electronic version]. Retrieved March 17, 2003 from EBSCOhost.

Minow, N. N., & LaMay, C. L. (1995). *Abandoned in the wasteland: Children, television and the First Amendment.* New York: Hill & Wang.

National PTA reaches consensus on TV ratings. (1997, July 10). [Press release]. Retrieved May 9, 2000 from http://www.pta.org/nycu/tvpr0710.htm

Pecora, N. O. (1998). *The business of children's entertainment.* New York: Guilford.

Sneegas, J. E., & Plank, T. A. (1998). Gender differences in pre-adolescent reactance to age categorized television advisory labels. *Journal of Broadcasting and Electronic Media, 42*, 423–434.

Universal Service Administration Company, Schools and Libraries (n.d.). Children's Internet Protection Act requirements. Retrieved January 19, 2003, from http://www.sl.universalservice.org/reference/CIPA.asp

CHAPTER TEN

Children's Programming

The children's entertainment and educational programming industry is the source of the messages we have been investigating. Along with the theoretical context we have used to guide our understanding, the variety of effects we have explored, and the mediation of parents, schools, and government, we now focus on the programming that is designed for children and the industry that produces the messages. We begin with a history of the relationship of the marketplace and children's media. Next we examine programs as case studies in the development of children's programming.

Children's programmers have found that those providing content for children's media can be most successful by listening to the children. Listening to children comes in many forms and a variety of research modes. To listen, a corollary is to be where children are. In media this has to do with distribution of the media messages. Distribution is done via the channels we have referred to in communication models; the messages are the content of the children's programs.

At least two ways media are coming together in the new millennium are (a) convergence of the media themselves in online Web sites, and (b) partnerships as seen in vertical integration, collaborative ventures such as Noggin, and international productions. These developments have contributed to changes in children's media and programming.

THE BUSINESS OF CHILDREN'S BROADCASTING AND CABLE

According to Pecora (1998), "Television has been described as a business that works on three simple principles: Keep the audience up, keep the costs down, keep the regulators out.... To this the children's television industry has added a fourth: Find someone else to pay the bills" (p. 3). Toys became that someone else. Almost from the beginning of broadcasting, toys have been connected to the industry's relationship to children. Although children's programming had household goods ads, toys were used as premiums by the household goods advertisers: "They all offered premiums and contests with rewards of toys, but, as a rule, toy companies did not advertise on radio" (Pecora, 1998, p. 11).

During the 1920s and 1930s, some of the major trends in children's consumerization were established: (1) the use of media markets to reach parents through children; (2) the application of "experts" and research to understanding consumer behavior; and (3) the targeting of food products and household goods to children, either to influence parents' purchases or to expand potential markets. (Pecora, 1998, p. 12)

Dick Tracy decoder rings and Little Orphan Annie mugs were highly valued premiums that showed a program and product tie-in. Collecting is important to children's developmental levels and advertisers have capitalized on this propensity by children to collect (Pecora, 1998).

Children's programming on radio grew from public service without advertising to include advertising.

On network radio, the number of hours of children's radio programming increased from 300 programs in 1930 to over 1,000 in 1933…. Many of these programs began without advertising, supported by the station, "to interest and entertain boys and girls, and at the same time satisfy parents."… As audience numbers and programming availability grew, product manufacturers took over program sponsorship. (Pecora, 1998, p. 25)

The same pattern of no advertising at first was also evident in broadcast and cable television. The advertising numbers climbed to over $1.3 billion in the year 2000: "More specifically, $1.08 million was spent during educational programs, $277 million during children's and family entertainment, and $860 million during animated fare" (Salfino, 2001, p. 16). As can be seen in these numbers, the educational programs have the least advertising dollar support. Educational programmers looked elsewhere for support because advertising would detract from their service to children.

Case of Children's Television Workshop

For public television, partnerships of program developers and program distributors helped to finance early quality children's television. The partnerships of early children's television can be seen in the Children's Television Workshop (CTW) and the Public Broadcasting System (PBS). When CTW and PBS joined forces, it was without advertising in a broadcast, over-the-air-dominated media world. CTW provided the content or message and PBS provided the distribution or channel. Sesame Workshop (formerly CTW) Chief Executive Officer Gary Knell said the two groups help each other: "We help them and they help us. They distribute our programs to 300 stations. We give them great content. And that formula has been sort of around now for 30 years" (G. Knell, personal communication, June 2000).

The partnership of CTW and PBS, however, needed further economic support that was at first provided by government funding. However, there was no guarantee that the funding would continue. Economically, the relationship has worked in part because CTW developed nongovernmental sources for funding.

> When Congress established the organizational structure for PBS in the late 1960s, a long-term funding base was never authorized. Consequently, as government support declined, stations have turned to nongovernment sources that look suspiciously like audiences (subscribers) and advertisers (foundations and underwriters). (Pecora, 1998, p. 100)

In addition, extensive licensing of products with their popular cast of *Sesame Street* characters allowed a secure economic base for CTW: "Character licensing is an agreement that allows the right to use a name or image in exchange for a royalty fee (generally 5–15% of the wholesale cost of an item)" (Pecora, 1998, p. 55). It began in the 1980s when commercial television rules changed and programmers began to partner with toy manufacturers. "Shows were developed with the consultation, and in some instances, financial backing, of toy manufacturers and licensing agents" (Pecora, 1998, p. 34). *The Smurfs* and *He Man* marked the beginning of the link between programming, advertising, and toy manufacturing. As in the case of CTW and licensing of toys for programs such as *Sesame Street*, the connection with toy manufacturers extended the life of toys tied to programs. However, licensing also served the programmers because it extended the television character popularity, keeping interest alive with children who play with the toys at home (Pecora, 1998).

Sesame Workshop head Knell says character licensing that began in the 1980s is crucial.

> Most not-for-profits, in fact, the bulk of our revenues come from licensing activities as well as foundation and corporate grants and international program sales to various distributors around the world. The basic economic equation is really around licensing and then licensing pays for our programmatic activities and research and content. (G. Knell, personal communication, June 2000)

Licensing as a revenue stream gave economic stability to CTW that was not consistently available from the government subsidies. That partnership still is working, but other partnerships such as the partnership with Nickelodeon in the venture called Noggin have been added and the landscape has changed. That new landscape is important to children's media because they want to be where the children are and the children are where the new media are.

Cable Television, the 1980s, Nick, and Disney

By the 1980s, children of Generation X and later Generation Y or millennials were watching cable television. Cable had joined broadcast television to provide children's programming and advertising. Because of the proliferation of channels on cable, entire channels could be dedicated to children's programming. Nickelodeon and Disney are two channels that took advantage of this opportunity.

Cable channels like Nickelodeon have a dual revenue stream. That means that not only do they get advertising revenues, but they also get subscription fees from the cable operator, who gets them from the cable audience. The advertising for cable could also be more focused because the viewers were a narrower portion of the audience and could program for a smaller population, like children. With the dual revenue stream, cable channels like Nickelodeon can make the economics of children's programming work.

Nick started as "Pinwheel" on Qube, the interactive cable experiment in Columbus, Ohio, in 1979 (Pecora, 1998). Nick moved to New York City in 1982 and was not advertiser supported at first, with 13 hours of programming daily. Nick was free of commercials for 4 years, but within 1 year of the move to New York, Nick had ads. Nick went to 24-hour programming in 1985. Nickelodeon moved to a commercial model with more animations and commercial tie-ins (Pecora, 1998). In addition to the dual revenue stream, Nick uses character licensing like CTW. The advertising includes some products Nick has developed. Green Slime shampoo was among the first of the Nick products: "Nick products are not always program related but often are products that encourage creativity and skill using the Nickelodeon imprimatur" (Pecora, 1998, p. 93).

The brand of each channel is an important identifier as to who they are and whether children and parent will use the channel. Nickelodeon competes, for example, with Disney and must differentiate who it is from Disney. Nickelodeon's Bruce Friend, Vice President of Worldwide Planning and Research, said the mission of Nickelodeon is to "Keep it contemporary and real" (personal communication, June 2000):

> Relative to Disney, we're very different. Disney's very much about the fantasy, the big fable or story. We never set out to be another Disney. It's important that we maintain a point of difference from Disney. We're about the contemporary family. We're about real life. (B. Friend, personal communication, June 2000)

In this way Nick differs from Disney, their biggest competitor for children's entertainment.

Disney was on cable in 1985. The Disney Channel, a premium channel, is funded by subscriber fees. Disney remains ad free but many believe the channel is just a long ad for Disney: "The stable of Disney stars receives exposure in multiple venues—motion pictures, television, audio- and videotapes, computer software, and books—and all are found on licensed merchandise" (Pecora, 1998, p. 89).

Three of the oldest children's television channels, PBS, Nickelodeon, and Disney, have tried to do without ads, but Pecora (1998) did not think any have succeeded due to the profit system that we live in. Few other options were provided in a capitalist system to provide the capital needed for research and development.

Initially, the Nickelodeon channel was commercial-free but within a few years turned to advertising for working capital. Public broadcasting has always set the standard for quality children's programming, and continues to do so, but now reflects the product-oriented shows of commercial television; the advertising-free environment of a Disney Channel is in fact one long commercial for Disney. PBS, Nickelodeon, and the Disney Channel become the brand names that readily identify a place for children's entertainment. (Pecora, 1998, p. 110)

The branding of these channels is critical to their financial success, but each also serves children and that means listening to them. Sesame Workshop and Nickelodeon do this listening through research and interactive venues.

LISTENING TO CHILDREN AND TEENS

Case of *Nick News* and Nickelodeon

Listening to kids means using their voices and their ideas. *Nick News* is the only news show in the United States for elementary and middle-school-aged children age 8 to 13. *Nick News* is produced by Lucky Duck Productions, owned by journalist Linda Ellerbee and her partner Rolfe Tessem. Nickelodeon contracts Lucky Duck to produce the news show that runs at 8 p.m. every other week on Sunday nights and 6 a.m. Wednesday mornings without ads for use by schools. The show has repeat showings on the Noggin Network, a joint venture of Nickelodeon and Sesame Workshop (formerly CTW). In *Nick News*, the kids are telling the story themselves, according to producer Mark Lyons. Listening to kids by using their voices helps *Nick News* to achieve its mission.

> One of the big ideas behind Nick News is to let kids be part of the dinner table conversation in current events so they can be in the loop on these things, because none of this stuff is so complicated that kids can't understand it. They just need to be told what's going on and they need to be told in their own language. (M. Lyons, personal communication, June 2000)

One segment of the show is titled "See What You Think." "We try to do pieces where we let kids exercise their choice muscles, where we give them an issue where they could find themselves easily on either side because the arguments are so convincing" (M. Lyons, personal communication, June 2000).

Another segment called "Mouth Off" is a soapbox for kids. "We just throw questions up and try to get a feel for where they come down," Lyons said. "That could be stuff on gun control, death penalty, bike helmets, anything where you ask, 'Where do you stand on this?'" Mail is another way *Nick News* listens to kids. The special titled "What Are You Staring At?" about persons with disabilities came from such a letter. A segment called "My Back Yard" also receives a lot of mail from kids who want to be on the segment to show something interesting in their neighborhoods.

Lucky Duck produces *Nick News* with distribution on both Nickelodeon and Noggin, a commercial-free channel sponsored by Sesame Workshop and Nickelodeon (see more on Noggin later). Nickelodeon fulfills its mission of being a kids' network. Even at the vice president's level, Nickelodeon is listening for children's voices. Vice President Friend does focus groups himself:

> There's no better way. I could sit here in this office and think I know anything about kids, and have all this kid stuff on my shelves, and read up on all these magazines and trades, but hearing it firsthand and seeing how they dress, what they're saying, what they're doing (works best). (B. Friend, personal communication, June 2000)

For Nickelodeon, it is their business to know what is happening with children: "We are the conduit to the audience. I represent the audience. You want to know what's going on with kids? You want to know if this is something that's going to play well with them? We should be able to tell you that" (B. Friend, personal communication, June 2000). They find that out by listening at all levels.

Case of Research and *Sesame Street*

Listening at all levels means knowing your audience and their developmental level. The program that has done that well for over 30 years is *Sesame Street* (see Fig. 10.1). For over 30 years the show's mission has been to prepare kids for school and now that preparation must take place earlier. When *Sesame Street* began (See "The Beginning of *Sesame Street*"), the target audience was 3- to 5-year-olds and now their target is 2- to 4-year-olds, as pre-kindergarten is now required in many communities. *Sesame Street* is for preschool children and the children are comfortable there:

> This is a show they feel embraced by and they are engaging with, because curriculum wise it is for them. It deals with them as a whole child and it does lay the foundation of early learning and a foundation of the love of learning. (R. Truglio, personal communication, June 2000)

Longitudinal research does show that *Sesame Street* fulfills its mission and children are better prepared for school, even into high school. Research done on *Sesame Street* indicates positive short-term effects on cognitive skills and long-term effects up to high school performance with higher grades in English, math, and science. Although research shows that *Sesame Street* can have a prosocial effect, that finding is less consistent than the findings on literacy and school readiness (Fisch, Truglio, & Cole, 1999). The research points to several trends including a wide range of effects that endure over time with consistency across cultures and even across generations of children for more than 30 years.

Research is an important listening element in the success of *Sesame Street*, where children's attention to the visual is tracked along with their behaviors. Truglio measured visual attention to the show, but more important she and her staff watch how children behave:

> Are they singing along? Are they moving to the music? Are they calling out the words? Are they saying the letters? Are they saying the alphabet? Are they asking questions? Are they labeling? All those behaviors are coded plus their verbal dialogue. Are they talking to their friends about what they just saw? (R. Truglio, personal communication, June 2000)

After the coded observation, Truglio does one-on-one interviews with the children, asking cognitive questions about comprehension and plot as well as affective questions about what they liked and did not like about the show. All that information then informs the next production. For example, in a typical 2-year cycle of programming by theme, the first year's research will inform the second year's productions. Purely exploratory research, however, may be when Truglio and her researchers are looking for ways to develop their curriculum. For example, when they develop an "Elmo's World" segment on balls, shoes, or games, they go out to talk to children:

FIG. 10.1.   Cookie Monster is featured online as well as in the long-running *Sesame Street* program © 2003 Sesame Workshop. Illustrations provided by Sesame Workshop.

We would go to daycare centers with small groups of kids and just talk to them about these topics, topics that they're interested in, to find out what topics we should explore that came from the kids, that's a part of their life. And then zeroed in on topics to find out what their thoughts are within this particular topic. (R. Truglio, personal communication, June 2000)

Research is an ongoing commitment even for an older show like *Sesame Street*. Sesame Workshop head Knell says the commitment to research continues to grow: "It's kind of like a pharmaceutical in the sense that we need to be doing basic research on illnesses, why they exist, and then research on cures which is content" (G. Knell, personal communication, June 2000).

The Beginning of *Sesame Street* As Told by Research Director Rosemarie Truglio

From the very beginning they knew that they wanted a show that would be entertaining, educational but entertaining. The show was never intended to replace the classroom. The intention was to give children, disadvantaged children, an opportunity to learn the basic academic skills or the basic school readiness skills to prepare them for kindergarten, because they didn't have access to more formal forms of education, daycare or preschool. But it was supposed to be zany and funny and that's where the Muppets come in. So that they wouldn't even be realizing that they were learning, because they were having so much fun. Also from the very beginning they wanted to make sure that parents would watch with their children because of the importance of extending these educational messages beyond an hour television viewing experience. That's why *Sesame Street* is written on two levels. (R. Truglio, personal communication, June 2000)

Case of Research and *Blue's Clues:* The Magic Sauce

Blue's Clues, like *Sesame Street*, is aimed at preschoolers. *Blue's Clues* is a game show for preschoolers that uses a live host who speaks directly to the audience, an animated game marker called Blue who reveals clues for the audience, and various props including a thinking chair and a notebook (see Fig. 10.2). *Blue's Clues* appears on the daypart called Nick Jr. on Nickelodeon. The same show is cablecast 5 days for a week of viewing the same episode. The mission of the show is "To empower, challenge and build the self-esteem of preschoolers all while making them laugh," Research Director Alice Wilder said (personal communication, June 2000). Blue is an animated dog that leads the preschoolers, with the help of a live host, through a game of guess what the answer is, similar to a game show. For *Blue's Clues* creator Angela Santomero, the parents are there because they want their children to have fun. "That's what we also get from parents is, 'It's just so sweet. It just talks so well to

Blue is a puppy only in her physical attributes;
her personality and actions mirror those of a preschooler.
She's irrestible to both kids and parents. Blue is playful,
affectionate, imaginative, curious and ready to learn.
Blue eats her cereal with a spoon and colors with crayons.
Blue created the signagure game of "Blue's Clues" that she
plays by leaving her trademark paw print "clues" for the
audience to find. Blue leaves three clues in every episode.
She also provides the driving energy for the show, both
because of her spirit and because each episode is about
figuring out what she needs or wants to do. The audience
may not realize right away that Blue is a girl; she has no girl
identifiers (bows, long lashes, etc.).

FIG. 10.2. Blue is an animated game marker for the *Blue's Clues* game show for
pre-schoolers. 2003 Viacom International Inc. All rights reserved. Nickelodeon, Nick Jr.,
Blue's Clues and all related titles, characters and logos are trademarks of Viacom International Inc.

my child. I'm amazed at the way my child interacts with it. So I really want to watch
that'" (A. Santomero, personal communication, June 2000). Being focused on the
children and their learning and enjoyment is one way parents are drawn in. Second,
Santomero said, parents are part of the target audience right along with children.
(See Santomero's description of the beginning of *Blue's Clues* later.)

Research Director Wilder says research is the key to success for *Blue's Clues:*

> Overall Nick Jr. knows they have something with research. They call it the "magic
> sauce." I really believe it (research) is only one of the elements that makes this show
> so successful, but they (collaborators on *Blue's Clues*) think that having the show so
> informed by kids is what is important to them. (A. Wilder, personal communica-
> tion, June 2000)

Children in the research phase see each episode of *Blue's Clues* three separate times. For each episode, the researchers first go to the children at the second draft stage of the script. Wilder and her researchers take the script and act out the show for a variety of children. They use drawings and pretend to be the host of the show. For example, in the episode titled "'Let's Boogie,' we actually acted it out," Wilder said. The feedback can also be children's verbal responses to what is presented, depending on the content of the episode. At this level, there are many changes that can be made to the script because it is still very flexible.

The second research stage is not quite as flexible because the host's performance is now on video. Changes can be made to the animation and music, but not the host's performance. This second time the researchers observe children is called the *video test*. Because the host is directly addressing the audience, it is critical that the children's interaction with the process is real for them. "When kids say to me in the school, 'I think he (the host) hears me,' those kinds of things are based on the fact that we do know what they (the children) are going to say," Wilder says regarding her research and developmental approach.

The last time children in the research phase see the episode it is complete and ready for television. There are no changes at this point. However, the researchers use this test to inform future productions. Wilder calls this the *content analysis stage*. Examples of the third viewing affecting future shows include changing the pace of the music, which was too fast, and changing the introduction to the thinking chair: "At first they had, 'And now we're ready for ...,' but children said notebook instead of thinking chair, so they changed the lead in to, 'And now we're ready to sit in our....' And now kids say, thinking chair," Wilder said (A. Wilder, personal communication, June 2000).

Research done on the show indicates the television strategy of showing each episode to the audience 5 days instead of one showing a week increases the confidence children have as indicated by their increased interactions while viewing:

> The episode repetition strategy improves comprehension while holding attention and increasing audience participation. As children watch *Blue's Clues* over months and years, their liking for the program increases, and the program has a beneficial cognitive and social impact, as measured by testing and caretakers' impressions. This suggests that the benefits to cognitive development that come from watching *Blue's Clues* are both cumulative and durable. Given the program's large audience, it appears that the program is not only doing well, but it is also doing good. (Anderson et al., 2000, p. 192)

The Beginning of *Blue's Clues* As Told by Creator Angela Santomero

When I was working around Nickelodeon within the development department, they wanted to do a game show. People were pitching things that were pretty typical of game show genre and yet it was for 2- to 5-year-olds. So I really kind of thought about that in relation to the kind of work I had been doing on play behavior and learning and teaching and really how preschoolers learn through games and through their own play. So I sat down and just talked about ideas I would have for taking this concept of a game show for preschoolers further and really to push it to education and learning and curriculum and a way to get at sequencing and colors and whatever.

And so I had formulated at the time more of a research report of how you would do this, how this game play would work and curriculum and all this and Brown Johnson who at that time was the senior vice president of Nick Jr. had said, "Conceptualize it more. Sell it to me more as a TV show. This is a research report more. Tell me more what you're thinking." So I did and it was literally 2 days later. I just went and thought about it more character-based and things like that and started to apply my learning. And I went back to her with ... more of the philosophy and the game play. And I had a preschool character at the beginning and a little animated character, just kind of the foundation of some of the thinking, but there was definitely a grain of the vision in there....

All of the game play and Blue came from the animated character. We really wanted a character that was preverbal that kids could relate to, the game piece in a way that could take you to the different areas to learn things. We wanted a live-action person because we really felt (there is) a strong connection (when) someone, especially someone older, asks for your help. The interactivity came from the active participation that we really wanted to see.... If you ask them something, they'll talk back to you. How can we do that more? All of the details really came from that foundation. (A. Santomero, personal communication, June 2000)

LISTENING TO PARENTS

The Case of *Nick News*

Coviewing of parents and children is a goal for many shows but sometimes parents are not watching and they let their children watch because they trust *Sesame Street* or they trust Nickelodeon. They trust the brand. That trust can make the producers sensitive about subjects that might offend parents. *Nick News* provides news without violence:

> If we're going to talk about people that are violent, we may show somebody being handcuffed and put in a police car. We're not going to show somebody shooting somebody. There's no need for that. You can get it without showing it. (M. Lyons, personal interview, June 2000).

Nick has won awards for covering some of the tough topics, including President Bill Clinton's impeachment, the war in Kosovo, and prejudice. For the impeachment story they focused on the danger of the president being removed from office and not the Lewinsky affair.

> We have to be able to figure out a way to do it so that Nickelodeon wouldn't be perceived as misusing the trust that they've been given. We walked that delicate ground with that Clinton and Monica Lewinsky thing and I think we pulled it off well. We were able to explain that there was a problem without going into the lurid details. (M. Lyons, personal communication, June 2000)

However, there are subjects *Nick News* has not covered due to that same trust. Hate crimes related to gays have not yet been covered, although the subject was considered when Matthew Shipp was killed. Lyons said the subject was discussed with Nickelodeon, but they decided to hold. There were several questions that had to be answered first:

> It will happen. It's just a question of how we'll do it. How's everybody in the corporate culture going to be happy with it? And how are we going to be happy with it? And how would we present it so that the parents would be able to make the choice and turn it off and not walk into a room and have a show on that they didn't know about and be furious? It's one of those things. (M. Lyons, personal communication, June 2000)

However in June 2002, *Nick News* did a special on gay parents titled "My Family Is Different." Everyone was not happy with the subject for children, but it is one way in which homosexuality impacts children. The special included a variety of viewpoints including a segment by Jerry Falwell, children who were religiously against homosexuality, and 13- to 15-year-olds being raised by gay parents. The show ran at 9 p.m. instead of its usual 8:30 p.m., with the suggestion that it was targeted for the older part of its demographic, those 12 and up. No advertising could be pulled because these specials run without ads (Salamon, 2002).

Concern for parents extends to covering subjects that parents may consider the parents' domain and governed by their values.

The Case of *Sesame Street*

Keeping the trust of parents is critical for any children's programming, but serving children is the focus. Executive Producer of *Sesame Street* Michael Loman said the long-term goal of *Sesame Street* is "to teach children how to live in today's world" (personal communication, June 2000). He said *Sesame Street* is the only show for preschoolers that does this. He said they do not use negatives. Instead, they ask questions and express empathy. For example, Luis is fixing Zoe's (3-year-old) mobile. Usually Maria would do this because it is her fix-it shop. Zoe is impatient and says, "I wish Maria was fixing it. She's faster." Luis responds, "You hurt my feelings." This expression of hurt allows children to understand that a person will feel hurt if they are treated that way. *Sesame Street* shows all kinds of children. Loman said they try to break both racial and gender stereotypes. They teach how to get along and how to respect the rights of all people (M. Loman, personal communication, June 2000).

Research Director Truglio reviews every script and watches the show in production with a monitor in her office. (The production is done in a studio in Queens, but the offices are in Manhattan.) Sometimes, however, there are mistakes and the measure of a show for children can be what is done about the mistake. Truglio recalled a show about tying a ribbon around a finger to help to remember something:

> Then the Muppets got a little crazy and put ribbons around their bodies. So on the script form I said, "please make sure to avoid head and neck." I did my job, but there must have been a meeting going on when we weren't watching the monitor. And so a segment got taped where Elmo had ribbon around his neck and it got aired and we got a phone call from a parent and I said, "No, they must have been watching some other show" because I checked the script. So I brought it to the attention of the producers. (R. Truglio, personal communication, June 2000)

The production was pulled after one airing. The producers of *Sesame Street* want parents to watch with their children to extend the learning of the educational messages beyond the 1-hour viewing. Another way of extending learning and viewing is with new media and new partnerships.

NEW MEDIA: THE "BIG X FACTOR"

In what Knell called the second wave (the first wave was cable television), the Internet companies have created an even broader landscape for children's media. The Internet is the new place that kids are and Sesame Workshop wants to be where the kids are.

> You have everybody from space.com on the science side to all these nature groups trying to invent themselves, magazines and all these media crashing together now so you don't have any more of this one TV box that has four channels. You now have this kind of converging media that's got thousands of choices. (G. Knell, personal communication, June 2000)

This world of interactivity also means internal reorganization of companies like CTW, which has changed its name to Sesame Workshop, a company organized to extend its message through a variety of media to reach kids wherever they are.

FIG. 10.3. "Elmo's World" is featured both online and as a special segment in the long-running *Sesame Street* program. © 2003 Sesame Workshop. Illustrations provided by Sesame Workshop.

We just reorganized our company to combine all of our content pieces under one executive.... Television and interactive software and online and magazines and books are now all going to be supervised by one area.... When we come up with new creative ideas they can be blown through all these different media so that we are going to get the kids wherever they are. A lot of people are talking about that and we're now doing it. (G. Knell, personal communication, June 2000)

Getting a message in a number of media is called *intertextuality*. For Sesame Workshop, the mission is educational content. For Nickelodeon the mission is to entertain the contemporary family with the focus on children. For both, the focus is on increasing distribution with their own content both in the United States and internationally, as discussed later.

Nickelodeon's Bruce Friend called technology the "Big X Factor." Children are drawn to new technology and are quick to learn it:

Kids by nature are very curious and exploring and technology at least in media is giving them a clear way to do that. We've seen this in the last 4 to 5 years with the

Internet and even cable television becoming more global and all. These mediums are like a window to the world. Kids, while they are still based in the home, have this incredible resource now to go out of the home and to really explore their world and to see the world around them and to see all of this stuff. (B. Friend, personal communication, June 2000)

To keep up with kids, Friend said Nickelodeon needs to be everywhere kids are, including the Internet:

We have to be everywhere in kids' lives having an impact. Whether that be buying a toy or the Big Help and trying to do something prosocially, it's not just about the business. We believe what's good for kids is good for business. It's not just about giving them TV shows that sell advertising. It's about hopefully enriching their lives. (B. Friend, personal communication, June 2000)

To promote what is good for kids, the business of children's media has crossed brand lines to create new partnerships.

NEW PARTNERSHIPS: NOGGIN

In the 1990s CTW wanted a better foothold on distribution in addition to PBS. The commercial broadcasters did not seem to understand the value of children's programming as they fought the battles against the CTA.

The commercial networks at the time didn't get it at all. They just buried educational programming as a ghetto and stuck it on at 5:30 in the morning and said "Look nobody's watching it. We were proven correct." So we just went there and fought those battles. And they didn't get it and they didn't want to get it. (G. Knell, personal communication, June 2000)

Then CTW started looking for better distribution and found a partner that had cable distribution and was looking for more educational content. They found their match with Nickelodeon and the Noggin network and Web site where both Nickelodeon and Sesame Workshop programming now runs.

We just said to ourselves, we'd better find a partner who does get it and who is willing to invest in building a new platform for kids that's educational in nature. Nickelodeon, it just so happened at the time, was developing their own philosophy about educational programming. Because they felt that they'd sort of gained such a huge market penetration, such a huge place for kids in the entertainment genre that they felt that they could sort of pivot into the education market as a different branding strategy. And they came up with the whole concept of Noggin independently before we showed up on the scene.... So we gave birth to this thing called the Noggin ... as a digital cable play, which would have an online component as well. (G. Knell, personal communication, June 2000)

CTW and Nickelodeon launched Noggin in January 1999 as a commercial-free joint venture. Noggin is a Web site and a television channel. Their Web site describes their origin this way:

> The people who make
>
> *Blue's Clues, Doug* and *Nick News* thought that the stuff that Children's Television Workshop made was really cool.
>
> Meanwhile, at the VERY same time ...
>
> Children's Television Workshop, the people who make *Sesame Street, 3-2-1 Contact* and *The Electric Company* thought the stuff that Nickelodeon made was really cool.
>
> So ...
>
> They decided to put their NOGGINS together to make a whole bunch of NEW and DIFFERENT COOL stuff ... and they decided to call it ... NOGGIN.
>
> The end. (Noggin, 2000)

INTERNATIONAL MARKETS

Noggin has not yet gone international, but both Nickelodeon and Sesame Workshop individually are expanding into the international market. Nickelodeon programming has been sold in more than 100 countries and broadcasts in close to 30 languages. Nick has channels in Europe including the United Kingdom (beginning in 1993) and more recently added Hungary in 2000. Nickelodeon is available to 23 Latin American countries in Spanish (started in 1996) and Portuguese (Brazil in 1998). The Asia/Pacific area was included beginning in Australia in 1995, Japan in 1998, and New Zealand in 2000. The Middle East was launched in 1996 and Africa most recently in 1999.

Case of *Blue's Clues* and "Total World Domination"

Blue's Clues has done particularly well on the international scene. "We have an aggressive international department because we want to reach as many kids as possible around the world with our curriculum, self-esteem and empowerment," Santomero said (personal communication, June 2000). "Total World Domination" is written on the whiteboard in the seminar room for *Blue's Clues*. Although the graffiti was supposed to be a tease of their many plans, the show has done very well internationally because it is designed to travel. The show is layered such that the host can be removed and another local host can easily be integrated electronically into the show. In the United States, there is a dubbed Spanish version that runs in markets like New York City. "If it's teaching human behavior, it will have positive value and it's going to be appreciated and therefore adopted by other marketplaces," Friend said (personal communication, June 2000).

Case of *Sesame Street* and Indigenous Coproductions

Sesame Workshop has a longer history with working internationally than does Nickelodeon. They have a two-pronged approach. One model has grown in the developed world:

> We're in countries like Germany, the UK, Canada, Australia, Spain, Holland and those places are pretty self-supporting. We also have licensing activities in those countries like we do here that spin off some revenues to support those ventures with *Sesamstrasse* products in Germany. (G. Knell, personal communication, June 2000)

In the developing world, the money for the programming must be philanthropically raised. Sesame Workshop has developed shows on conflict resolution for Israeli and Palestinian children. Sesame Workshop raised $6 million for the Israeli–Palestinian coproduction.

Sesame Workshop builds indigenous coproductions with the partner country. They do not simply dub the U.S.-made show into the language of the partner country:

> The point on that is that we've always stood for being an entity that doesn't just take an American show and dump it into Mexico or to Brazil or to China. We actually work in those countries directly with local producers and writers and artists, teachers, and educators and the ministry of education to build indigenous coproductions of our work. (G. Knell, personal communication, June 2000)

One of the productions Sesame Workshop is working on now is in Egypt on a project focusing on girls in education there.

In South Africa the funds have come from a combination of the U.S. Agency for International Development and a major corporate sponsor, the biggest insurance company in South Africa, Samlam. In addition, Sesame Workshop also received in-kind donations of airline tickets from South African Airways to work on the production called *Takalani Sesame*. "But it's really patching together those kinds of corporate, foundation and government grants to make it all work," Knell said. "You can't really support that with a market-driven perspective."

Because South Africa has 11 official languages, the show there is creating multilingual characters that use more than one language. *Takalani Sesame* is the first sub-Saharan production of Sesame Street and the 20th international spin-off. In addition, *Takalani Sesame* is the first *Sesame Street* to include a radio component (Singer, 2000).

> Just as *Sesame Street* was started 31 years ago here, we think in a country like South Africa it can have almost a bigger impact there than the original show did in this country. It started to bridge the educational gaps that exist with a majority population that's been disenfranchised historically. (G. Knell, personal communication, June 2000)

As of September 2002, *Takalani Sesame* has an HIV-positive character. The purpose of the character is to educate children about AIDS. The government made the request because one in nine South Africans is HIV positive for a total of 4.7 million South Africans, more than any other country. The female Muppet is an orphan (Associated Press, 2002).

Knell explained that Sesame Workshop has found a formula for working with other countries on these coproductions:

> So you take a show that's *Sesame Street* and it's not just about a U.S. show with U.S. characters. But it's about kids who look like me and grownups who look like my parents and talk like my parents. And we see a diverse country like India in front of us with all of its amazingly rich cultural issues and languages and different ethnic groups and religions and all that stuff. And you begin to sort of embed in little kids sort of an appreciation of where they are and an introduction to the real world. I don't think at least in our lifetime that that need is going to go away. (G. Knell, personal communication, June 2000)

Partnerships are critical to the viability of projects abroad as well as the continued development of children's media at home.

BOTH PARTNERS AND COMPETITORS

Although Sesame Workshop and Nickelodeon have come together as partners with Noggin, they also are competitors. Sesame Workshop's *Sesame Street* is after the same audience as Nickelodeon's *Blue's Clues*. Vertical integration has created other partners in children's television. Disney's purchase of the ABC network has led to an ABC block with Disney programming on Saturday morning. Viacom, the parent company of Nickelodeon, has merged with CBS and is going to have a Nick Jr. block on Saturday morning. Thus, "The consolidation in the media industry has actually ironically helped the qualitative equation in children's television unintentionally," Knell said (personal communication, June 2000). More quality programming is getting on television from the stronger providers such as Disney and Nickelodeon.

> Disney, one could argue, is not a household word in education, but it certainly is a household word in quality programming and safe programming for kids. They've taken that over and actually done a couple of educational shows and they've got a pretty nice schedule now that works. It's popular. It's pretty good stuff. Science Court, some other shows they have are educational, they work. (G. Knell, personal communication, June 2000)

The partnering may have strengthened children's programming from some points of view, but it has made the landscape a bit more confusing. "You can't look at the world anymore as us versus them. It's kind of where do you exist, and be true to your cause, and pick alliances where they work for you" (G. Knell, personal communication, June 2000).

Children are a minority we can all relate to because we have all been there. Children are the one minority that becomes a majority each generation. Their relationship to the mass media will continue to evolve as the generations change and new mass media dominate for each generation. As we look to our future and the challenges we will face as professionals, parents, and community members, we can play a role by understanding the complex way in which the issues of children, teens, families, and the mass media must be considered.

SUMMARY

A variety of sources and partnerships bring the new landscape of programming on a variety of channels and platforms to children all over the world. Partners have forged relationships creating new programming options while continuing to compete with each other. It is ironic that vertical integration has meant not only that there are fewer owners, but there also is more sharing within these corporations of programming, which works well for children. The key to success is listening to children through research and other feedback. The key to working in the world is listening to the needs of individual countries as well in indigenous coproductions. Creative, collaborative, and caring listening and ideas are the key to the future of children and media.

RESOURCES ON THE WEB

- *Blue's Clues* Web site at http://www.nickjr.com/bluesclues/home.html
- *Nick News* Web site at http://www.nick.com/all_nick/tv_shows/shows.jhtml?propertyId=239
- Noggin Web site at http://www.noggin.com/index_content.tin
- *Sesame Street* web site at http://www.ctw.org/

REFERENCES

Anderson, D. R., Bryant, J., Wilder, A., Santomero, A., Williams, M., & Crawley, A. M. (2000). Researching *Blue's Clues*: Viewing behavior and impact: A research synthesis essay. *Media Psychology, 2*, 179–194.

Associated Press. (2002, July 15). This Muppet is HIV positive. *The Keene Sentinel*, p. 15.

Fisch, S. M., Truglio, R. T., & Cole, C. F. (1999). The impact of *Sesame Street* on preschool children: A research synthesis essay. *Media Psychology, 1*, 165–190.

Noggin. (2000). What's Noggin? Retrieved July 11, 2000 from http://www.noggin.com/whatsnog/11 July 2000

Pecora, N. O. (1998). *The business of children's entertainment*. New York: Guilford.

Salamon, J. (2002, June 18). Children, gay parents and synthetic storms. *New York Times*, p. E1.

Salfino, C. S. (2001, March 5). Tykes, tweens & teens: Room for all in TV's fun house [Special report]. *Broadcasting and Cable, 131*, 10, 16–22.

Singer, R. (2000, August 4). Big Bird in South Africa. *Christian Science Monitor*, p. 7.

Glossary

Acquisitions Model: A media literacy approach that aims to help children develop those skills to create media including photography, videography, and web page development.

Active Audience: Young viewers and listeners who use the media as part of their own socialization.

Active Mediation: Talking to children about mass media messages using categorization, validation, and supplementation.

Adaptive: A generational profile characteristic of action that brings people together across generations, finding common ground for action.

Adolescence: A developmental stage characterized by egocentric and risk-taking behaviors without concern for consequences.

Advertising: Any message intended to encourage buying a product.

Aggression: A forceful action that confronts people or their ideas (short of violence).

Bullet Theory: The mass media theory that states the message goes directly and without interference from the source to the receiver.

Character Product Licensing: The link between programming and toy manufacturing by which program characters become toys for which the programmer receives a royalty fee paid by toy manufacturer.

Chicken and the Egg: Refers to the question: What came first, the chicken or the egg? In research, it indicates the problems of identifying the true cause of an event such as violence. Is the person predisposed to violence or does media violence cause the behavior?

Child Online Protection Act (COPA): Passed in 1998, Congress replaced CDA with COPA in an effort to regulate indecency on the Internet. Referred to as CDA II, the Congress made the new act narrower in its applications, trying to recreate the successful standard community standard found in the *Miller v. California* case that still is used today to evaluate decency for broadcast media. In June 2000, the Third Circuit Court of Appeals found COPA unconstitutional. COPA is still under appeal.

Children's Internet Protection Act (CIPA): In this third attempt to regulate indecency on the Internet, Congress required filtering to protect children as they access the Internet at school and in public libraries. The act required libraries to use filtering software in order to continue receiving government funding. The U. S. District

Court found the act unconstitutional but the decision is being appealed by the government.

Children's Online Privacy Protection Act (COPPA): Passed in 1998, Congress provided this legislation to protect children under the age of 13 from invasions of privacy on the Internet. Children's web site operators must both give notice that they are collecting personal information and get parental permission to do so.

Children's Television Act of 1990 (CTA): The first United States federal law regulating children's television and requiring both education messages and a limited number of advertising messages.

Civic: A generational profile characteristic of action as a group for the common good.

Cognitive Processes: Ways people acquire and develop knowledge.

Cognitive Strategies: Verbal explanations or instructions.

Cohort: A contemporary in time by reason of birth dates close in time.

Commercials: Advertising found on radio and television.

Communication Decency Act (CDA): The act is part of the Telecommunications Act of 1996 and tried to regulate indecent language on the Internet, but was found unconstitutional in 1997 for the Internet provision.

Communication Model: A diagram that shows the relationship of the elements of communication as it occurs: source, channel, receiver, message, feedback, and noise.

Concept-oriented: Family communication patterns that encourage a variety of viewpoints as the highest value.

Content Analysis: A systematic examination of the message of the communication. The content analysis can say nothing specific about the effects the message might have on the receiver.

Convergence: The coming together of the various mass media in one unit on the Internet.

Core Programming: The FCC term for educational/informational programming that fulfills the CTA requirement for educational programming.

Coviewing: Watching mass media with children but without any rules or conversation.

Creativity: Presentations original and meaningful to others.

Cultivation Analysis: An examination of how television's worldview matches the worldview of heavy viewers of television.

Developmental Reciprocal Theory: A very specific developmental theory by Eron & Huesmann (1984) that provides the specifics of the reciprocal relationship between television violence and aggression in which viewing TV violence leads to aggression and more violence viewing that establish schemas or scripts for children whose behavior continues with aggression in their adult lives.

Developmental Theory: The theory or approach attributes children's abilities at certain ages to common characteristics based on their growth.

Displacement: When children choose to use mass media, they are not choosing other types of activity like playing outside with their friends, thus media are taking the place of those other activities such that they do not occur due to time spent with media.

2002 Dot-Kids Implementation and Efficiency Act: The law is the fourth attempt to protect children from indecency on the Internet. It side-steps content regulation issues by created a separate domain for children's web sites as part of the U.S. Internet domain. The law provides an Internet place for children's sites that would prohibit hyperlinks that lead users to other sites outside the domain. In addition, chat rooms and other forms of interpersonal communication that may allow sexual predators would be banned unless the site could be secured.

Dual Revenue Stream: In cable television, the ability of a cable channel to collect both subscriber fees and advertising for the same programming.

Factuality: Reality based on cognition.

Fantasy: That which is created by the imagination and does not exist in the actual world.

Fictional Involvement: A mediational device focuses the viewer's attention on the victims instead of the perpetrators of violence, thus immunizing them from imitating the violence.

Fictionalized News: Information presented as if it were news but created from fantasy.

Forbidden Fruit Effect: Children may be attracted to shows rated inappropriate for them by age or by content designation.

Formal Features: Specific visual and auditory production techniques that are the grammar of audiovisual messages.

Generation: People as a group of the same age.

Generational Theory: Each generation has its own characteristics and that four generational profiles go in cycles: idealist, reactive, civic, adaptive.

Home Utilities: A mass medium used inside the home including radio, television, and Internet.

Idealist: A generational profile characteristic of actions that aim toward some higher good or value beyond the everyday.

Imagination: The creation of something new that is not based on previous experience.

Indigenous Coproductions: For Sesame Workshop, the development of shows branded as *Sesame Street* in foreign countries by working with the people of that country on goals appropriate to their culture.

Inoculation Analogy (or Approach): The skills being taught in the media literacy program protect the child from negative effects.

Intertextuality: The same story line in a variety of media.

Macro Theories: Theories that examine the larger society.

Mass Media: Those channels of communication that reach the wider audience simultaneously with their messages.

Media Content Literacy: Media literacy in this model sees media as conduits that differ by form, but what is important is the content. Media literacy in this model is geared to analyzing content.

Media Education: School-based media literacy projects.

Media Grammar Literacy: Media literacy in this model is geared to how each medium works and how each medium's grammar can be analyzed. In this case the content is constant and not the focus.

Media Literacy: Having the skills to both "read," that is access, analyze, and evaluate, as well as "write," that is communicate in a variety of mass media.

Medium Literacy: Media literacy in this model goes beyond grammar to how the medium is used. Different skills are required to use various media such that literacy is not the same in each medium.

Micro Theories: Theories that examine the individual.

Millennial Children: Those who have a high school graduation date of 2000 and beyond.

Noncognitive Strategies: Showing or doing instead of explaining.

Premiums: Tokens included with products to encourage buying the product.

Program-length Commercial: A television show that has characters that are toys as well as TV characters presented with the purpose of selling the toys by promoting them in the program.

Protectionist Model: A media literacy approach that aims to shelter children from the evils of the mass media.

Ratings: A designation to show whether programming is appropriate by indicating the age for the target audience and / or the content included in the message.

Reactive: A generational profile characteristic of action motivated by the actions of earlier generations.

Reality: That which exists in the actual world.

Restrictive Mediation: Making rules for children regarding their use of the mass media.

Risk Composites: Locating types of programming with characteristics that might impact children at various ages and providing the relationship between the programming and the child by age.

Schema Theory (plural: Schemas or Schemata): Also called script theory, schemata theory states that the receiver will choose information that reinforces his / her attitudes or beliefs and assumes models, beliefs, and expectations constructed by the individual guide human behavior.

Social Inference: Basing understanding on the responses of others such as the behavior of teachers and other children.

Social Learning Theory: Predicts that children who watch will imitate the behavior they see on television by attention, retention, repetition, and motivation.

Social Realism: Reality based on motives for viewing and television experience.

Socio-oriented: Family communication patterns that encourage social harmony as the highest value.

Stereotype: Seen as a fixed or general pattern instead of as a variable individual.

Tainted Fruit Effect: Children may reject programming that is rated as inappropriate for them by age or by content designation.

Theory: A theory tries to explain and predict what will happen in certain circumstances under a given set of assumptions or conditions.

Three-hour Rule: A rule the FCC made to help define the CTA that states that all broadcast television stations must provide 3 hours per week of educational programming for children.

Variables: Those elements in an experiment that change depending on the action or characteristics of other elements.

V-Chip: A device that allows adults to block some programming on television from being accessible to children.

Violence: An action that goes over the limits of individual comfort by force of word or deed (greater than aggression).

Author Index

Subject Index

A

Action for Children's Television (ACT), *see* Child advocacy groups
Advertising, 15–16, 23, 30, 42, 69, 148, 168 *see also* Gender
  business of children's broadcasting and cable, 154–158
  CTA, 140–143
  consumer socialization, 99–100
  deregulation, 138–139
  developmental age, 25–26
  gender images, 95–99
  media literacy, 124–125, 130–131
  program-length commercials, 62–63
Audiences, *see also* Family, Media literacy
  active, selective, 4, 24, 107–110, 113–114, 121–122, 164
  empowering, 14–16, 29, 61, 120, 128–129, 161

C

Cable, 156–158, *see also* Programming
  Disney, 156–158
  dual revenue stream, 157
  Nickelodeon, 156–158
Center for Media Education (CME), *see* Child advocacy groups
Child advocacy groups, 138–141
  Action for Children's Television (ACT), 15, 138–140, 151
  Center for Media Education (CME), 140–141, 151
  Children's Television Act of 1990, *see* Law

Cognitive processes, *see* Perceptions
Communication model, 5–7
  generations, 33
  research, 72
  theories, 8–9, 11
Creativity, 24, 32, 61–63, 73, 157

D

Development of children, 4
  fears by age, 51–52
  media perceptual characteristics by age, 25–31
  preschoolers (ages 2–5), 19, 21, 25, 75, 161, 164–165
  children (ages 6–12), 4, 6–8, 25–27, 78, 106, 158
  teens (adolescents), 4, 11–12, 19–20, 27–32, 43, 57, 68, 73–74, 77, 81–82, 94–97, 107, 110, 112–113, 123, 126
  news event response by age, 53–57
Diversity, 81–88, *see also* Theories
  ethnic minority images, 89–93
  gender, 93–95
  identity, 93–95

E

Effects and media images, *see also* Theories
  concerns, history of, 67–72
  eating disorders, 81, 96–97
  obesity, 83
  sexuality, *see* Gender